...rtan carpet balls • mocha ware • treenware • bandboxes • folk art plates • cocktail shakers • cobalt glass
chairs • 1940s vases • doll beds • vintage trunks • old postcards • carved hands • toy ... • missouri pine
globes • roseville pottery • red wing pottery • bluebonnet pottery • landscape painti...
...ooks • state plates • swizzle sticks • japanese ikebana baskets • architectural fragments • ...
sculptures • japanese antiques • italian seating • theatrical posters • automata • victorian books • magic sets
...niture • wedgwood pottery • barbecue trays • mexican kitsch • red-clay dinnerware • monterey furnishing...
wood carvings • stone carvings • painted walking sticks • beaded suits • redware pottery • wooden signs
... • face jugs • shoshona stonework • painted sticks • easter baskets • depression glass • tarnished silver
...rnival chalkware • royal copley pottery • tole trays • staffordshire pottery • majolica • english transferware
...s • nutcrackers • mccoy pottery • maple syrup cans • oil paintings • vintage textiles • antique cupboards
...ctorian carpet balls • mocha ware • treenware • bandboxes • folk art frames • cocktail shakers • cobalt glass
...t chairs • 1940s vases • doll beds • vintage trunks • old postcards • carved hands • toy robots • missouri pine
globes • roseville pottery • red wing pottery • bluebonnet pottery • landscape paintings • texas biedermeier
...ooks • state plates • swizzle sticks • japanese ikebana baskets • architectural fragments • looking glasses
sculptures • japanese antiques • italian seating • theatrical posters • automata • victorian books • magic sets
...niture • wedgwood pottery • barbecue trays • mexican kitsch • red-clay dinnerware • monterey furnishings
wood carvings • stone carvings • painted walking sticks • beaded suits • redware pottery • wooden signs
... • face jugs • shoshona stonework • painted sticks • easter baskets • depression glass • tarnished silver
...rnival chalkware • royal copley pottery • tole trays • staffordshire pottery • majolica • english transferware
...s • nutcrackers • mccoy pottery • maple syrup cans • oil paintings • vintage textiles • antique cupboards
...ctorian carpet balls • mocha ware • treenware • bandboxes • folk art frames • cocktail shakers • cobalt glass
...t chairs • 1940s vases • doll beds • vintage trunks • old postcards • carved hands • toy robots • missouri pine
globes • roseville pottery • red wing pottery • bluebonnet pottery • landscape paintings • texas biedermeier
...ooks • state plates • swizzle sticks • japanese ikebana baskets • architectural fragments • looking glasses
sculptures • japanese antiques • italian seating • theatrical posters • automata • victorian books • magic sets
...niture • wedgwood pottery • barbecue trays • mexican kitsch • red-clay dinnerware • monterey furnishings
wood carvings • stone carvings • painted walking sticks • beaded suits • redware pottery • wooden signs
... • face jugs • shoshona stonework • painted sticks • easter baskets • depression glass • tarnished silver
...rnival chalkware • royal copley pottery • tole trays • staffordshire pottery • majolica • english transferware
...s • nutcrackers • mccoy pottery • maple syrup cans • oil paintings • vintage textiles • antique cupboards
...ctorian carpet balls • mocha ware • treenware • bandboxes • folk art frames • cocktail shakers • cobalt glass
...t chairs • 1940s vases • doll beds • vintage trunks • old postcards • carved hands • toy robots • missouri pine
globes • roseville pottery • red wing pottery • bluebonnet pottery • landscape paintings • texas biedermeier
...ooks • state plates • swizzle sticks • japanese ikebana baskets • architectural fragments • looking glasses
sculptures • japanese antiques • italian seating • theatrical posters • automata • victorian books • magic sets
...niture • wedgwood pottery • barbecue trays • mexican kitsch • red-clay dinnerware • monterey furnishings
wood carvings • stone carvings • painted walking sticks • beaded suits • redware pottery • wooden signs

mercury glass • roadside pottery • majolica • french transferware • looking glass • 1930s white pottery • ch
1939 world's fair memorabilia • bakelite jewelry • mies van der rohe furniture • lucite handbags • seashells •
northwest indian carvings • santos • dog memorabilia • bauer pottery • french dinnerware • haeger potter
horn furniture • native american weaving • rosemaled bowls • metal banks • vintage glass • action figu
southern antiques • architectural drawings • windsor chairs • totem poles • primitive masks • ceremonial bo
photographs • mission furniture • heywood-wakefield furniture • glass paperweights • 1950s italian glass
geometric rugs • western oil paintings • wagon wheels • bottle cap sculpture • psychiatric-patient paintin
cigar-store indians • weather vanes • commercial tins • game boards • beadwork • ceremonial masks • carv
sheet music • red transferware • white dinnerware • figurine pairs • heywood-wakefield furniture • rumrill
bamboo furniture • victorian shell art • cookie jars • orange glass • cigarette boxes • silhouettes • animal
mercury glass • roadside pottery • majolica • french transferware • looking glass • 1930s white pottery • ch
1939 world's fair memorabilia • bakelite jewelry • mies van der rohe furniture • lucite handbags • seashells •
northwest indian carvings • santos • dog memorabilia • bauer pottery • french dinnerware • haeger potter
horn furniture • native american weaving • rosemaled bowls • metal banks • vintage glass • action figu
southern antiques • architectural drawings • windsor chairs • totem poles • primitive masks • ceremonial bo
photographs • mission furniture • heywood-wakefield furniture • glass paperweights • 1950s italian glass
geometric rugs • western oil paintings • wagon wheels • bottle cap sculpture • psychiatric-patient paintin
cigar-store indians • weather vanes • commercial tins • game boards • beadwork • ceremonial masks • carv
sheet music • red transferware • white dinnerware • figurine pairs • heywood-wakefield furniture • rumrill
bamboo furniture • victorian shell art • cookie jars • orange glass • cigarette boxes • silhouettes • animal
mercury glass • roadside pottery • majolica • french transferware • looking glass • 1930s white pottery • ch
1939 world's fair memorabilia • bakelite jewelry • mies van der rohe furniture • lucite handbags • seashells •
northwest indian carvings • santos • dog memorabilia • bauer pottery • french dinnerware • haeger potter
horn furniture • native american weaving • rosemaled bowls • metal banks • vintage glass • action figu
southern antiques • architectural drawings • windsor chairs • totem poles • primitive masks • ceremonial bo
photographs • mission furniture • heywood-wakefield furniture • glass paperweights • 1950s italian glass
geometric rugs • western oil paintings • wagon wheels • bottle cap sculpture • psychiatric-patient paintin
cigar-store indians • weather vanes • commercial tins • game boards • beadwork • ceremonial masks • carv
sheet music • red transferware • white dinnerware • figurine pairs • heywood-wakefield furniture • rumrill
bamboo furniture • victorian shell art • cookie jars • orange glass • cigarette boxes • silhouettes • animal
mercury glass • roadside pottery • majolica • french transferware • looking glass • 1930s white pottery • ch
1939 world's fair memorabilia • bakelite jewelry • mies van der rohe furniture • lucite handbags • seashells •
northwest indian carvings • santos • dog memorabilia • bauer pottery • french dinnerware • haeger potter
horn furniture • native american weaving • rosemaled bowls • metal banks • vintage glass • action figu
southern antiques • architectural drawings • windsor chairs • totem poles • primitive masks • ceremonial bo
photographs • mission furniture • heywood-wakefield furniture • glass paperweights • 1950s italian glass
geometric rugs • western oil paintings • wagon wheels • bottle cap sculpture • psychiatric-patient paintin

Collector's Style

BETTER HOMES AND GARDENS BOOKS®
Des Moines, Iowa

Collector's Style

Editor and Art Director: Richard Michels

Executive Editor: Denise L. Caringer

Contributing Writers: Catherine Hamrick, Candace Ord Manroe

Contributing Editors: Andrea Caughey, Laura Hull, Nancy Ingram, Sylvia Martin, Barbara Mundall, Hilary Rose, Mary Anne Thomson

Contributing Photographers: Gordon Beall, Edward Gohlich, William Hopkins, Jon Jensen, Mark Lohman, Sylvia Martin, Alise O'brien, Peter Walters

Copy Chief: Terri Fredrickson

Copy and Production Editor: Victoria Forlini

Editorial Operations Manager: Karen Schirm

Managers, Book Production: Pam Kvitne, Marjorie J. Schenkelberg

Contributing Copy Editor: Sherry Hames

Contributing Proofreaders: Judy Friedman, Heidi Johnson, Beth Lastine

Indexer: Kathleen Poole

Electronic Production Coordinator: Paula Forest

Editorial and Design Assistants: Kaye Chabot, Karen McFadden, Mary Lee Gavin

MEREDITH® BOOKS

Publisher and Editor in Chief: James D. Blume

Design Director: Matt Strelecki

Managing Editor: Gregory H. Kayko

Director, Operations: George A. Susral

Director, Production: Douglas M. Johnston

Vice President and General Manager: Douglas J. Guendel

BETTER HOMES AND GARDENS® MAGAZINE

Editor in Chief: Karol DeWulf Nickell

MEREDITH PUBLISHING GROUP

President, Publishing Group: Stephen M. Lacy

Vice President-Publishing Director: Bob Mate

MEREDITH CORPORATION

Chairman and Chief Executive Officer: William T. Kerr

Chairman of the Executive Committee: E. T. Meredith III

The Collection Obsession

For me, the collecting addiction began with one small brightly glazed flower pot. This single pot was soon joined by one, then two more pots in a variety colors, patterns, and shapes. Twenty-two years and 58 McCoy pots later, my first collection fills the primitive blue cupboard shown on the cover of this book. (The rest of our house begins on page 150.)

My collection obsession has continued and now includes a dozen midcentury collections, such as Heywood-Wakefield furniture, Royal Copley pottery, and even bowling balls. My favorite finds have become a focal point of our home's eclectic decorating style. But when I started collecting, I soon learned that displaying collections wasn't as easy as acquiring them. Was I the only one with this decorating dilemma? I searched magazines and books to see what other collector's had done with their treasures. Never did I find a book or magazine dedicated to showing collectors' homes. Perhaps there were too few collectors like me?

A few years ago, I read a newspaper article that explained the growing collecting trend. "One-third of Americans are active collectors," said the writer. At that point, I realized that I was far from alone in my collection obsession.

Collector's Style is for all of us who are proud of our collections and want them seen in our homes. In this book you will find a variety of collecting styles. But most importantly, you will see how to decorate with these collections you love.

Rich Michels, Editor & Art Director, Collector's Style

Contents

Introduction

The formula for collector's style is simple: Let your passion lead the way! Dispense with strict decorating rules and play with objects of the heart—whether you're a seasoned collector or just discovering your magnificent obsessions. With *Better Homes and Gardens Collector's Style,* you'll discover the power of collectibles as an integral part of decorating.

On every page—packed with fresh photography and expert information—you'll experience firsthand

CREATING
Collector's
Style

collectors' strategies for displaying pieces to their best advantage. Each of the five chapters represents a particular decorating solution.

If you're challenged by large quantities of objects, Chapter 1, "Massing Your Collections," explains how to organize particular groupings. The approach may be tight or loose, depending on your preference.

Perhaps variety spices your life; however, managing

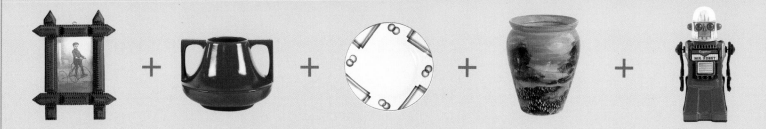

myriad styles and furnishings may seem akin to a precarious juggling act. In Chapter 2, "Mixing Your Collections," learn how easily you can accommodate all manner of period pieces in the same space—whether opting for a conservative, bold, or even outrageous interior design statement.

Items amassed over years can overwhelm even a large area. If your house looks cluttered, take control. Chapter 3, "Editing Your Collections," shows how to select from a number of objects and rotate them periodically. That way, you'll enjoy your collections while conveniently, and inexpensively, transforming the look of a room.

Some individuals view their collections as fine art. To display your prize pieces as if worthy of a gallery, turn to Chapter 4, "Collections As Art." Here you'll find innovative ways to present pieces dramatically while avoiding the atmosphere of an institutional setting.

The final chapter, "Color Choices for Collections," will help you choose the colors for walls, floors, upholstery, and furnishings that will best complement your collections—soothing neutrals, easy-on-the-eyes pastels, or hues bursting with energy.

Each chapter has a focus, but you'll find rich variety throughout the book. The sheer range of collections, from high art to kitsch, fascinates: pottery, stoneware, porcelain, glassware, souvenir plates, chrome, pewter, silver, mirrors, boxes, baskets, toys, shells, metal banks, matchbooks, posters, tiles, action figures, jewelry, handbags, blankets, rugs, textiles, snuffboxes,

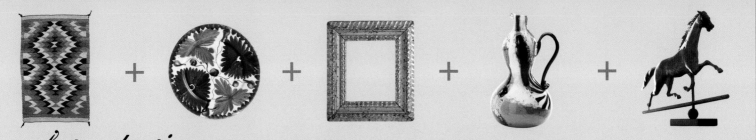

Introduction

architectural fragments, walking canes, ash trays, sculptures, paintings, folk art. . . .

This book represents more than a list of things. It's about people too—fellow collectors. Chances are, you'll meet a kindred spirit, someone who also collects the things you love. Whatever their collections, these homeowners share their expertise, punctuated by anecdotes, quips, and wry commentary. Also tucked in every chapter are clues about shopping for, evaluating, and maintaining collectibles.

Collectors with a flair for decorating are a breed apart. Certainly, they're drawn to the dynamics of the hunt—the anticipation, the act of combing flea markets and shops for the elusive find, and the triumph of holding the quarry in their hands.

The experience does not end with acquisition, however. What collectors *do* when they bring their finds home also brings joy and delightful dilemmas. Antiques dealers Darwin Otto and Brent Heeb, whose story begins on page 12, are a case in point. They collect a lot of everything, which would not be an issue if their house had a few thousand square feet to spare. Darwin and Brent, however, are limited to 1,500 square feet, and they like to showcase masses of treasures: roadside pottery, white florists' vases, folk art dotted with buttons and seashells, transferware, clocks, and more. These gentlemen pull off decorating in tight spaces with aplomb. Count their den—small with the illusion of airiness—a work of genius. Opting for a white-on-white scheme, they lined a mix of

 +  +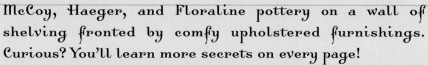

McCoy, Haeger, and Floraline pottery on a wall of shelving fronted by comfy upholstered furnishings. Curious? You'll learn more secrets on every page!

Think of *Collector's Style* as an engaging journey to singular homes. You'll travel to each coast, as well as distinctive regions, such as the South, the Midwest, and the Southwest, exploring an array of architectural settings: 18th- and late 20th-century townhouses, farmhouses, modest bungalows and coastal cottages, midcentury and contemporary ranches, a downtown loft in a New South city, and suburban dwellings in colonial, Norman, California Mediterranean, and other styles.

Once you step inside, the fun truly begins! The 20 featured houses are celebrations of colors, patterns, and textures coordinated—and sometimes intriguingly contrasted—with various furniture styles. You're sure to find clever ways to enhance how you decorate with collectibles, whether your taste tends toward Federal restraint, Victorian ebullience, sleek modern, wild eclecticism, or the shabby chic of loose slipcovers and distressed woods.

Collector's Style is not an armchair road show, but rather a call to action. Imagine how you might arrange your own collections. Be adventurous! Experiment with unexpected nooks to set off prized pieces. Lavish color on a wall or create a monochromatic backdrop. Suddenly, you'll see the familiar from a fresh perspective. Decorating with what you adore adds up to pure pleasure— an inspired lesson for any space, anytime.

 +  +  +  +

Chapter 1

Thank goodness BIRDS OF A FEATHER flock together: The world looks *less cluttered* that way! The same principle applies to decorating. No matter how much YOU LOVE THEM, *collectible treasures* can ride roughshod over your best decorating intentions unless they are HERDED TOGETHER in some way. When *your collections* threaten to run amok, cast yourself in the role of a decorating cowboy: Saddle up

Massing Your Collections

and *prepare to herd* your favorite things into cohesive groupings following these two simple DECORATING RULES:

● CORRAL LIKE OBJECTS in their own special places, instead of allowing them to *wander all over* the house. DISPLAY COLLECTIONS together on a shelf, on a table, or on a wall.

● ORGANIZE DISPARATE objects by color—say, all green or all white pottery—to *avoid a cluttered,* catchall look.

mercury glass

roadside pottery

majolica

french transferware

looking glass

1930s white pottery

Between the two of them, ANTIQUES DEALERS Darwin Otto and Brent Heeb collect a little—*make that a lot*—of everything. In their Portland, Oregon, TOWNHOUSE, they hold NOTHING BACK. Shiny mercury glass shares a room with matte *swirl-patterned* roadside pottery. A *profusion of vintage* white florists' vases makes way for clusters of memory jars—FOLK ART PIECES studded with COSTUME JEWELRY, seashells, and buttons. Old New

+ + =

England paper boxes and clocks mingle with transferware and LEATHER BOOKS. The smorgasbord is enough to whet almost anyone's appetite. What *makes the home* most IMPRESSIVE, THOUGH, is how the owners do it. In just 1,500 square feet, they manage to turn this *all-over-the-place* plenitude into orderly, EYE-PLEASING ARRANGEMENTS. *Their secret?* Tightly knit groups of like objects. Some span entire walls; others gather on a SINGLE SHELF.

CLUSTER AND CONQUER

A wall of shelving in the den is devoted to all-white pottery that's a mix of McCoy, Haeger, and Floraline. Against white walls and juxtaposed with white-upholstered furnishings, the display looks clean despite the large number of pieces.

Collecting is a *social* activity—it gives a focus to travels and *shopping*

Colorful roadside pottery sold as souvenirs outside national parks and landmarks in the 1920s features bold swirls. Its placement keeps the eye moving from the mantel to a fireside table to the pair of iron-and-glass coffee tables.

Brent and Darwin don't tolerate "less is more" for a minute. Their collections-rich decorating style flies joyously in the face of modernism's favorite credo. Unlike many collectors, they don't cull out the keepers, hanging onto only the best or most valuable pieces. Quite the opposite. "We collect when things are cheaper, because then you can get masses of them—enough to make them look important," says Brent. "It's the masses that matter to us."

It's been years since they've sold a personal collection, and they don't trade up. "We just add," says Darwin. He disdains the thought of stashing collections in boxes, even for rotational display.

"What's the sense of collecting if it's all hidden away?" Darwin says.

Order does somehow prevail. Darwin and Brent's displays prove that massing multitudes of like objects can create harmonious and endlessly interesting interiors. Consider their abundance of white vintage pottery. Common sense says the numbers should pose a classic decorating display problem, but no. Instead, a herd mentality of sorts provides the solution: Displayed on two walls of shelving in the den, the white pottery looks orderly and uncluttered. The pieces work together to form a single decorative element, covering the walls almost like a subtle patterned paper or fabric, or a decorative paint treatment. Brent and Darwin's displays may

inspire other collectors to rethink their approach: Consider adding to—not subtracting from—a collection to give it enough clout for a major massed display.

Not every collection needs or merits an entire wall. In fact, most of Darwin and Brent's collections are confined to smaller quarters. Mercury glass, which Darwin started collecting years ago "because it was so inexpensive," brings a shimmer to the small built-in shelves on each side of the fireplace in the living room. Filling one bookcase with the collectible mandated filling the other to match. It's all about balance: Symmetrical shelving dressed with a single

above: Circa 1890 Chippendale-style frames with their original mirrors bring continuity to the stairway. To knit together the space, the reflective look is repeated with mercury glass that is arranged on a nearby blue cupboard.

collection provides the visual continuity that keeps both sides of the room in balance.

Mercury glass, with its reflective surface, is so low-key that it serves as a backdrop for more graphic collections. Any neutral-colored collection, in fact, makes a good companion for more busily patterned objects. In Brent and Darwin's living room, streaky roadside pottery provides color and bold pattern that contrast beautifully with the mercury glass. Placed on the mantel and tabletops, the pottery also helps weave together the conversation area. Note how smaller items, such as those on the mantel, gather together for the most design impact. Larger collectibles, such as the vase on the fireside table, stand alone.

Darwin and Brent have mastered the art of grouping collectibles by object type, by color, or by texture. For example, a cluster of candlesticks and other antiquities shows off on the den's French commode, while antique Chippendale-style mirrors climb the stairwell wall together.

Vintage pottery—all green—blankets bedroom shelving. Collections of colorful dinnerware are stacked together in the kitchen—not just for looks, but also for accessibility because the dishes are meant to be used.

One of the most interesting examples of massing is the dining room, where built-in shelves turn a disparate array of treasures into a personality-filled focal point. The eye-catching grouping includes vintage clocks, folk art memory vases made from keepsakes, an irresistible jumble of old leather books, wallpaper-covered boxes, a wooden chest, and small mirrors. The objects are compatible because they share gold and yellow colors, as well as worn textures.

The display's blend of old and new—aged objects massed on sleek, architectural shelves—is repeated by the table and chairs. Chic and simple, the wicker chairs echo the golden tones of the collectibles. Similarly, the table appears thoroughly contemporary until one gets close enough to appreciate the aged patina of its metal base.

Clean-lined shelves display a diverse collection of well-worn treasures, all linked by golden tones that repeat in the wicker chairs. The sleek table, crafted of glass and aged metal, reinforces the room's intriguing blend of rustic and refined.

Bright walls, vivid chipped-paint wicker chairs, and an iron table make good companions for the kitchen's colorful mix of vintage potteries. **opposite:** An all-green collection of Floraline and Haeger pottery reinforces the serene bedroom palette.

"Collecting is an acquiring thing for us probably an obsession, but a very good one."

19

groupings, clockwise from above left:
Combining like items creates order. Brent and Darwin's displays include a large Mexican bowl filled with assorted custard cups, transferware and hand-painted bowls, memory jugs, and mercury glass vases with faint painted designs. The large lidded hand-painted Talavera urn is from Mexico. Pottery groupings add interest throughout the house: Majolica, roadside pottery for which they've paid anywhere from a few dollars to several hundred dollars apiece, and colorful painted 1930s Ranburg pottery from Indiana, which is displayed on counters and cabinet tops.

In Search Of The Ugly Duckling

Beautifully stylized swan-shaped pottery, such as this cream-colored vase, was made by most of the major pottery companies in the 1930s. This particular piece is unmarked, but Brent says it doesn't matter to his kind of collecting: "I'm looking for the aesthetics, not a specific pottery." Likewise, chips or blemishes are no big deal if your goal is aesthetics versus investment. "When you're buying a round bowl for under $10, an imperfection doesn't matter," says Brent. Most of the larger pieces in Brent's collection currently sell for $20 to $50 or more. Antiques malls are his favorite "one-stop shop" for finding pottery.

Strike While Mercury Is Hot

Darwin's mercury glass collection started with a lucky tip: "After a woman came into my shop and said that 'one of these days this stuff will be worth something,' I bought a piece out of self-defense." Made in the 19th century as an inexpensive alternative to sterling, mercury glass features two glass walls with the inner wall coated with a silver color. Originally, but not for long, mercury was used for the inner coating, thus, the glassware's name. A metal or glass disk sealed the bottom hole through which the silver coating was applied. If the disk is missing, the glass may tarnish or become damaged, especially if water seeps between the inner and outer walls.

Wayne Fisher is a PERSISTENT HUNTER and gatherer of old things in a *new century*. Perhaps his greatest find is his 18TH-CENTURY TOWNHOUSE in Alexandria, Virginia, AN appealing *historic district* on the southern edge of Washington, D.C. It's HARD TO IMAGINE, but for more than 70 years the structure *suffered from* neglect until RESCUED BY LOCAL preservationist Joan Haley, who furnished it with American *country antiques*. A

connoisseur *of Americana*, Wayne has filled his 2,000-square-foot home with an INTRIGUING ARRAY of collections. Dollhouses and birdhouses perch on pedestals. BASKETS OVERFLOW with Victorian carpet balls. Tramp art and treenware crowd tabletops. *Mocha ware* and other pottery types *line the shelves*. Yet this dealer who is mad for antiques has a method to KEEP CONTROL: grouping pieces by *similarity, contrast,* color, or proportion.

QUIRKY AMERICANA

Wayne often groups objects by theme. Fascinated by miniature buildings, he places dollhouses and birdhouses near each other. Signage tops a symmetrical backdrop of architectural fragments, shutters, and folk art frames.

right: Wayne seeks out primitive 19th-century portraits and landscapes, as seen in this area of the living room. A salvaged fireplace mantel surrounds a painted desk from Pennsylvania. **far right:** Game boards and stoneware jugs dress up the stairway.

In the living room, an oversize ledger serves as a base for Victorian carpet balls, a tramp art trinket box, and woodenware. Wallpaper-covered boxes stacked beneath the table were one of Wayne's earliest collecting passions.

Wayne Fisher's American Design, a by-appointment shop with a clientele from California to Maine, houses only the finest quality Americana, but the dealer lightens up at home. "I don't necessarily want an assemblage of trophy pieces at home," he says. "It means a whole lot more to take ordinary objects and put them together in an extraordinary way."

Like most collectors, Wayne clusters similar objects and experiments to create themed arrangements. He also takes pleasure in creating visual tension between collections. For example, he might juxtapose smooth with rough surfaces or contrast folk art with fine art.

Tucking objects in unexpected places is yet another way to heighten interest. For instance, a salvaged mantel appears to encase an antique secretary. A ship rests on a window ledge instead of a shelf. Wayne even has a wool penny rug on his bed as a throw.

Anyone would expect to find an antique trade sign hung on a wall or suspended from the ceiling, he says; positioned from the floor, such a sign makes a novel statement.

In addition to wall space and floor space, he advises using built-in shelves, mantels, stair landings, and ceiling space to create visual layers. Wayne has positioned his stunning assortment of folk art frames in a stairwell that doubles as a gallery. At the heart of the arrangement are two "crown of thorns" frames.

Mixing and matching colors adds to the element of surprise. Victorian carpet balls of varying hues and patterns pile in baskets. A salesman's sample of a child's red sled punches up a subdued corner of black-and-white game boards and pale jugs.

Varying the scale of like objects—stacking different-size bandboxes, for instance—sets off pieces to their best advantage. Displays that mimic the proportion of architectural elements—such as the vertical lineup of two landscapes and a Chippendale mirror between two windows—also intrigue the eye.

Wayne doesn't hesitate to move around objects either. "When I bring in

something new, it can be like playing dominoes to find a place for it," he explains. "I don't want to showcase individual pieces. Every object is meant to play off another."

By necessity, immense collections require editing, which offers another opportunity to try something new. Before moving into his townhouse, Wayne sold scores of baskets. He not only lacked room for them, but he also realized that the sheer volume of his collection was detracting from his best examples. Besides, Wayne says, he can bear parting with some pieces because there are always more to be scooped up at the next show.

When shopping for personal treasures, Wayne goes for what pleases him, not others. For instance, he adores landscapes done by unschooled painters of the Victorian period, though they may not turn the heads of art lovers or even many collectors of country antiques. Still, he remains enthusiastic. "Victorians painted on all sorts of things with exuberance," he says.

If an object seizes your attention, go for it, urges Wayne. Upon finding a child's Pennsylvania slat-back chair, he instantly knew he wanted it. "I bought it right off a dealer's truck before the show even opened," he says. "You have to develop an instinct for what you better grab right away."

Yet in following his passion, Wayne is still particular. Condition counts, he says, but an item also should reflect its long history of use. Wayne always tries to buy only antiques that are authentic and unaltered.

Once in awhile, he goes against his own advice—and buys a stray piece because of its character. For example, he's made room in his house for a framed cut-paper Valentine with a missing piece. He also has hung onto an oil lamp repaired with a wooden base after its original glass bottom broke. Wayne looks for the human spirit in all that he collects, down to his humble memory jugs, which are decorated with buttons and other mementos of long-ago families' loved ones.

"I don't showcase *individual* pieces; every object is meant to play off *another*."

Intricate folk art frames can be hung as works of art in their own right. "Crown of thorn" frames, such as the two in the center of the display, are held together by interlocking pieces. To avoid a static look, Wayne mixes frames of different sizes.

above: Flanked by a pair of New England Windsor chairs dating from the 1790s, a painted blanket chest sports a menagerie of chalkware animal figures, naive figures that Wayne calls "poor-man's Staffordshire."
right: These colorfully patterned carpet balls, used in playing parlor games during the Victorian era, are piled in baskets. **left:** Treenware goblets, exquisitely shaped, show off natural wood tones and handmade patterns. **far left:** Tramp art candlesticks share a tabletop with a small needle case appliquéd with rosebuds.

Mocha Ware's Utilitarian Beauty

Mocha ware, fairly common in American homes 150 or more years ago, refers to the utilitarian yellowware (pottery made from buff clay) that is decorated with bands or wavy lines. The most common decorating technique of mocha ware involved slip banding. To make *slip*, the artisan mixed clay with plaster of Paris, combined it with a stain or flint, and applied it to the unglazed piece. Originally, the term *mocha* referred to the brown decorations applied to the pottery. Actually, white and blue colors also were used, with cobalt blue being the most popular. Feather quills or sponges used in application rendered designs that suggested natural forms, such as trees, earthworms, or seaweed. These pieces, functioning in the everyday world as mugs and pitchers, artfully brightened homes, just as they do those of modern-day collectors.

Tramp Art: Myth Vs. Fact

This term is a misnomer: Hobos hopping trains did not indulge in making these cunning pieces. Tramp art refers to a type of woodworking that gained a following in the late 19th and early 20th centuries in most industrialized countries. To decorate various objects, craftsmen, often home hobbyists, employed notch carving and layering of small wood pieces. They often used wood recycled from cigar boxes. To learn more about this craft, consult these references: *Tramp Art: One Notch at a Time* (1998) and *Tramp Art: A Folk Phenomenon* (1999).

There is no museum DEDICATED TO ART DECO and mid-20th-century *modern design* in Des Moines, Iowa. Sheree Clark's 1939 house is the NEXT BEST THING. Its Art *Deco architecture* with glass block, blond brick, and flat roof offers a hint of things to come. INSIDE, THE HOUSE sparkles with SHINY CHROME and brushed aluminum industrial houseware designs—*especially cocktail* shakers and coffee pots—and ARCHITECT-DESIGNED

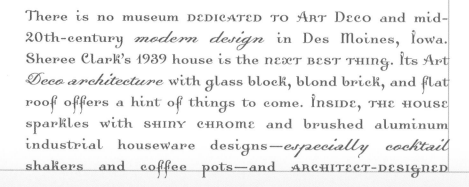

furnishings from the likes of *famed modernist* Ludwig Mies van der Rohe. A collection of Abingdon Pottery U.S.A. tulip vases gathers on a *window ledge;* wares by INDUSTRIAL-DESIGN giant Russel Wright dress the dining table. Art Deco rules, but UNDER ITS WING is every kind of collectible: 1939 New York *World's Fair memorabilia,* LUCITE HANDBAGS, metal compacts, and more. As Sheree's friends *have discovered,* one visit is never enough.

Indulging In Deco

Contrasting shapes engage the eye. Curvy Abingdon vases play against the dining room's hard edges. Steel-and-leather chairs by architect Ludwig Mies van der Rohe pull up to a table set with Russel Wright dishes, flatware, and glasses.

Sheree isn't joking when she says that design is her life.

"I literally live and breathe it," says the owner of a graphic design business. "Everything in my everyday life is about design. My home and office are filled with mid-20th-century pieces, especially ones from the 1930s. About the only thing I collect that's not period are posters and designs by my business partner, John Sayles." Even there, she's in good company. The firm's award-winning designs are shown in the Cooper-Hewitt National Design Museum, in The Smithsonian Institution, and in The Library of Congress.

People in the graphic design business have a reputation for an almost obsessive tidiness, and with it, a contempt for clutter. Sheree, the firm's managing business partner and not herself an artist, is no exception. She says she won't tolerate clutter. Yet an inventory of the number of individual collectibles in her home would be staggering. Her design secret? Vast collections of small trinkets, such as compacts, copper jewelry, plastic jewelry, cameras, 1960s wooden-and-rhinestone handbags (and even earlier Lucite handbags), abound. By carefully categorizing the collections, then grouping all of a kind together, Sheree has managed to preserve the streamlined quality that is the essence of Art Deco style

and of modernism in general. For instance, cobalt-and-chrome barware, topped with a selection of chrome and aluminum cocktail shakers and pitchers from various makers, imparts a unified countenance to a modern buffet and the glass block cubbies above it. Elsewhere, a glass block wall serves as a backdrop for a collection of multicolored vintage glassware by Blenko, one of the few remaining glass factories in America to still produce handblown modern production glass. Sheree's advice: Take advantage of a single wall or windowsill as an opportunity to mass a collection for the greatest decorative impact and the least cluttered look. Along the same line, her

Classic end tables include a chrome table at left, which holds a Comet coffee service by Chase, and a 1935 Wolfgang Hoffman table at right. On the mantel, Blenko glass flanks a mirror that reflects an A. M. Cassandre poster.

Tall Blenko glass vases and decanters dating from the 1950s and 1960s bring varied color to a glass-block window. The Blenko Glass Company, still in existence, has produced handblown glass for more than a century.

A **lively** **cast of small objects plays on a stage set by mid-century** *furniture* **classics.**

above: Heywood-Wakefield furniture lightens the look in the Florida room, where a mirrored wall of glass shelves reflects '50s Lucite handbags. **below:** Vintage bamboo pieces team beautifully with reproduction Mies van der Rohe armchairs.

furnishings—themselves a collection—are homogeneously grouped in every room, with lots of repeat appearances by slick, linear leather and chrome sofas and chairs.

It's in the sunroom at the back of the house where Sheree downshifts into a more casual style. Airy enough for a beach house, wicker and chrome furniture and blond, highly collectible Heywood-Wakefield pieces create an easygoing ambience.

Although the furniture lets the room function as an alternative living space, the Florida room's more important function is that of a repository for Sheree's smaller-size collectibles—hundreds and hundreds of them. Glass and wood department store display cases, true to the mid-century period and feeling, allow the eye to browse easily over treasures that are gathered together on the various shelves. One case is filled with copper jewelry, while wooden purses march along a high shelf. Also used in stores, metal jewelry rods—both standing and table models—are festooned with vintage bead necklaces.

The sunroom also proves that containment means control—and good design. In Sheree's home, confining potentially ungainly collections of small objects on tabletops, in glass-front cases, and on windowsills not only gives the collectibles a sense of place, but it also turns them into decorative focal points in the process.

Sheree's love of classic modern furniture pulls her entire home together. The bedroom sports stellar furnishings designed by 1930s modernist icon Donald Deskey, best known for his sumptuous interiors for Radio City Music Hall in New York. Plastic jewelry from the 1930s stands at the ready atop a Deskey vanity.

Those plastic bracelets displayed on her dresser aren't just for looks. Sheree wears them, thus living the collector's life to the fullest.

Sheree believes that no collection is ever "done"— at least not hers. "I travel so much for business that, wherever I go, I'm always on the lookout for more things to add."

In true *collector's* style, Sheree turns any surface into *display* space.

The top ledge of a glass-block wall displays only 1960s wooden handbags designed by Enid Collins. Display cases, such as the curved-glass department store Beauty Bar cosmetics counter on the right, are themselves collectibles.

above: Bedroom furnishings are by Donald Deskey, a 1930s designer best known for the interior of the Radio City Music Hall at Rockefeller Center in New York. **right:** A vintage department store display fixture hosts a casual showing of plastic bracelets on its glass arms. **left:** Grouped together, vintage compacts make a strong design statement. Sheree's compacts include those by Richard Hudnut, Coty, Volupte, and Evening in Paris. **far left:** With their unmistakable Deco detailing, Teague cameras paint a picture of classic modern design.

Is Compact, Will Travel

Compacts, such as this beautifully stylized Art Deco piece by Karess, left, and a souvenir compact commemorating the 1934 Chicago World's Fair, above, are welcome additions to Sheree's serious Deco collection. The Karess compact has never been used; its powder is blemish-free. Sheree began collecting compacts because they travel light. "No shipping necessary. Put them in your purse; you're on your way home," she says. Building on a theme, such as Art Deco, by displaying small items along with larger furniture pieces, creates a rich collection and a host of memories. As Sheree says, half the fun of being a die-hard collector lies in hunting objects on vacations and business trips and hauling them home as souvenirs. "Each time I travel somewhere, I try to steal a little time to antique, even if it's brief. A couple of extra minutes on a taxi ride to the airport can do it."

Hands Off The Chrome

The best rule for maintaining a high-gloss mirrored finish on chrome housewares, such as this 1930s-vintage Chase Brass & Copper Co. coffee urn from Sheree's collection, is to keep hands off. If children or pets live in the house, keep shiny metal collectibles out of reach: Cabinet tops make good perches. Even when out of reach and displayed for looks only, shiny metal housewares are subject to collecting a thin buildup of grime that hides their brilliance. Periodically, wash them in warm, soapy water. In between, remove fingerprints and smudges with a household mirror and glass cleaner and a soft cloth or chamois. Never use a paper towel; it can scratch the finish.

Guests at Tim and Carol Bolton's *weekend beach* house must WAKE UP SMILING when the sun rises on the Texas coast. The *blue-green* Gulf of Mexico sits just a STONE'S THROW from the thicket of greenery that cools the cottage. The setting is *blissful, uplifted* by the clear, SINGING PASTELS that Carol has chosen as her palette. If you're a baby boomer, you may *well remember* the happy yellow, green, white, and CARNATION PINK colors from the 1950s.

+ + =

The pastels stir up *warm-weather* memories—fat sticks of chalk and HOPSCOTCH COURTS, candy-coated almonds *slowly savored* through Saturday afternoon matinees, HOMEMADE LEMONADE, doll dishes, and pretend tea parties. The Boltons, who own *home furnishings* and ANTIQUES STORES in Fredericksburg, like to exchange their hardworking weekdays for MAGICAL WEEKENDS when they're surrounded by *light-hearted* collections.

COTTAGE BY THE SEA

A palette of clear *pastels* lends a festive
atmosphere to this *seaside* retreat.

left: The combined living and dining area picks up the pink, yellow, and green pastels of vintage containers. right: In the bunk room, vintage trunks and doll beds store folded linens. The walls are embellished with a map of an imaginary coastline.

It's hard to imagine, but this weekend retreat was once a cinder block fisherman's shack built in 1940. Despite its initial dilapidated appearance, the Boltons were drawn to the cottage.

"We knew the second we drove up that it could be perfect for us," says Carol.

Like seafaring souls setting off on a great adventure, the couple gathered courage and embarked. They raised the roof a bit to make higher ceilings. Then they turned to Carol's brother-in-law, Tom Proch, to collaborate on the interior paint finishes. He dreamed up the living and dining area's broadly yellow-striped walls and executed the pink diamond-patterned floor.

Carol's decision to use carnation pink was, at the time, a brave move. Nonetheless, she wanted to evoke pleasing midcentury pastels, which are echoed in collectibles tucked about the house.

Vintage pillows and fabrics—some strong on pink—strike a happy note stacked atop a painted green cupboard. In the kitchen area, pink shelves accommodate glassware and dishes that alternate buttery and blushing colors.

The swirling, curlicue lines of the dining chairs, which were copied from a Victorian antique, pick up on the airy-as-cotton-candy feel, as do the lace tablecloth and glass topping the table. In keeping with the casual mood, the yellow-and-white chandeliers were pieced together from odds and ends.

A nautical theme ripples throughout. Starfish and seashells swim among other collectibles on tables, from 1940s vases to old-fashioned postcards. Wall art includes a Gulf Coast fish-market sign, an old seascape from a New England restaurant, and even a map of an imaginary coast. Life preservers and a parasol function as pretty-in-pink props. Set off by seashell frames, artwork of past-period bathing suits line a weathered shelf.

In this festive atmosphere, the Boltons kick back, taking a deserved break from business. "We visit with friends we've invited or walk along the ocean," says Carol.

A trip to the Brimfield, Massachusetts, antiques fair inspired the name of the Boltons' cottage. The couple discovered an old graveyard sign spelling out "Fineview" in iron letters. They hauled the sign back to the coast and propped it near the front door, an appropriate christening gesture that suits their weekend home—inside and out.

clockwise from top: Garlands of antique milliner's flowers dress up lace curtains in the guest room, while life preservers reinforce the nautical theme. Old postcards and shells create a still life on a side table. Another still life continues the fresh air theme, with a vintage fan, pink-painted seashells, and 1940s vases. A small basket is put to alternative use as a bulletin board propped on a table. A short trip down the road turned up an intriguing find—a fish-market sign that offers a prominent view of a Gulf Coast shrimp boat.

Midcentury Fun
Recaptured And Contained

Some 20th-century pottery has continued to go up in price. Just ask collectors who have gravitated to McCoy, USA, and Bauer pieces. If you're looking for vases, pitchers, glassware, and other containers to add a cheerful note to tables and shelves, but are not interested in making a huge investment, head for a nearby flea market, antiques mall, or thrift store. You will find colorful wares that are plentiful and inexpensive. Pastel pink, yellow, green, or blue pottery also makes perfect accessories for a preteen girl's room.

Instant
Art Found In Postcards

Vintage postcards enhance a variety of settings. You can choose from so many themes—from floral-bedecked cards that recall your great-grandmother's youth to travel destinations. Tourist postcards from almost 100 years ago, such as those commemorating the World Exposition in St. Louis, sometimes come in sets. Some people enjoy collecting vintage postcards that bring warm memories of vacations in France, England, Italy, and other foreign locales. Old postcards make nifty souvenirs— and they're certainly easy to pack if bought overseas. What's more, they're simple to display in holders or under glass.

Chapter 2

Falling in love may be exhilarating, but what happens when the objects of YOUR AFFECTION run the style gamut, from Deco to Directoire? What if *your decorating* sensibilities embrace both THE SOPHISTICATED and the silly? Instead of thinking, "Uh-oh," give yourself a hand! After all, anyone can line up a litter of Staffordshire dogs *on a mantel,* but how many can create real decorating drama by mixing

Mixing Your Collections

it up? To start, choose a design *strategy* to suit your taste:

• PLAY IT SAFE. Mix pieces that fall within one palette (red, white, and blue; pink and green, *blue and yellow*) or one theme ("PARIS," "nautical," "floral"—even "round stuff").

• PLAY IT LOOSE. Let a bold-colored or large-scaled object take center stage. Mix TEXTURES—cool metals, rich woven rugs, silky fabrics—for drama. Toss in *the unexpected!*

The more Rick Ege TRAVELS AND LEARNS, the more his *collecting evolves*. After earning his degree in art history, he said no to graduate school and *an academia* job for one reason: TOO STATIC. He wanted change. Selling antiques meant travel—a *steady stream* of new people and places. It also meant being AROUND THE OBJECTS he's loved SINCE CHILDHOOD. From the seashells and rocks he collected with his grandmother, and *still displays*, Rick

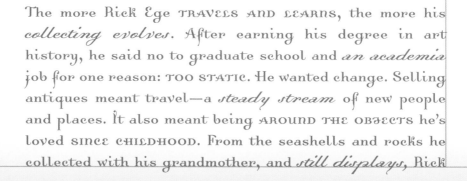

has evolved into COLLECTING ALL MANNER of folk art, including *carved hands*, sculpted faces, santos (saints crafted in Hispanic countries), and NORTHWEST COAST Native American artwork. *Rick collects* everything from DOG MEMORABILIA to American antiques—especially those from Missouri—as well as EUROPEAN PIECES. His collections are as broad as *his interests*. Want to get to know him? JUST SNOOP AROUND his St. Louis home.

An Evolving Eye

"Everything I *collect* is somehow an *expression* of me."

A large 1700s processional figure believed to be Mary joins a 1900 Missouri pine piece that holds a crowned slave carving from Tennessee. The head with a pill on its tongue is a 19th-century doctor's sign welcoming African-American patients.

Most zealous collectors will tell you they never finished adding to or upgrading their collections. Rick qualifies the statement, admitting that he has no problem letting one collection languish while in hot pursuit of another. The eclectic style that prevails in his home is not so much a conscious quest for diversity as it is an inevitability. It's how his mind works; his eye simply follows.

"I feel that the more you learn about objects, history, and the world, the more interested you are in a wide variety of things. It just clicks," Rick explains. "My collection changes over time. I'm influenced by the people around me— by what my friends see and collect. From travels to Europe, my collections have grown to include Continental pieces, as well as Americana."

Old and new worlds, childhood and adulthood, all converge in Rick's home. In his living room, a pair of 1920s French leather armchairs reflects his broadening interests as a well-traveled adult. The chairs huddle close to a large 19th-century copper church panel, which represents his lifelong affection for architecture. Sidling up companionably to the seating area are a few collectible dogs that trigger happy childhood memories.

The secret to Rick's style of eclecticism is that no single interest outweighs another. A new collection that reflects his latest travels and growing sophistication isn't allowed to encroach on those that came before. Seashells still decorate a bedroom; a toy robot collection represents the toys he admired but never owned as a child. His decorating is more "tell" than "show," revealing the story of his life instead of striving to visually impress.

"My interest in dogs comes from having them as pets throughout childhood," Rick explains. "Being on the road all the time, I can't have one now. That's why the dog collection has grown by leaps and bounds." In his typical egalitarian spirit, Rick welcomes all breeds in his collection, as well as all memorabilia.

The architectural panel feeds Rick's intellectual curiosity. "It has every

above: French leather armchairs from the 1920s face off in front of a copper church panel. Folk art pieces add warmth. below: Northwest Coast Native American carvings adorn an English chest. The framed basket is 19th-century Apache.

bell and whistle from 1880s architecture that you would want," he says. "The heart, crossed swords, flames, torches—everything that was grand—is in one panel." He adds that the panel represents more than architectural history.

"It was done by a coppersmith for his church," says Rick. "He was pouring his heart and soul into that piece, and it shows. That's what draws me to it."

Emotional content is present in most of his collections. Each room resonates with handcrafted reminders of humanity. Artists' model hands, heads, and human figures are abundant, along with folk art busts and figures. The more the artist is present in a piece, the better. His stylized crow decoys, he says, are hands-on evidence of their maker's understanding of "the streamlined essence of a crow, without getting lost in the details." Crows keep watch in the dining room, as well as over Rick's computer in his home office—a reminder of the importance of the human touch in a high-tech age.

Rick prizes his Native American art collection for similar reason: "It is spiritual," he says, as are his santos and other religious carvings. "The work has a depth that you don't see in work done just for profit. The same depth exists in a portrait of a dog done by its owner. It may not be a good academic painting, but it has a depth of emotional connection between subject and artist."

Emotional content means more to Rick than fair market value. "I have many pieces that are monetarily worthless, but they have immense value simply because they speak to me."

Rick's collections encourage anyone who wants to create an intensely personal style. The trick is to decorate with autobiographical pieces—objects that recall childhood and teens, as well as last week's discovery of beauty. The more inclusive collections are, the more singular the charm of a home. Seeking out such objects enhances a sense of well-being and brings a smile to every beholder.

Metal chairs used in institutions in the 1930s and 1940s and an antique French bronze chandelier contrast with the mid-1800s Missouri pine table Rick bought at age 18. Pine Kentucky columns frame a "THINK" sign from a school.

clockwise from top: A folk art crow decoy by Charles Perdeu perches on the desk beneath mixed collections of religious art. A dog painting by an anonymous folk artist points to shelves rife with dog collectibles, from collars to old photos. A 19th-century wooden articulated artist's model sits between artist's model hands. Old employee badges form a collection. A carousel horse head adds dimension to early German cow pull toys. Robot toys bring color to the guest room. The German Black Forest brackets are carved heads.

MUST HAVE MR. ROBOT, MUST HAVE...

Brightly colored plastic robots from the 1950s and 1960s are hot collectibles today. "I was always fascinated with them as a kid, and because I never got to own any then, I collect them now," Rick explains. He notes that prices have soared; those in his collection range from $150 to $6,000 each. "That's because these are mint. Plastic toys don't usually last long, and there weren't that many of them made to begin with," he says. Those that survive with all parts and paint intact are pricey. A light dusting with a feather duster is all they need. No cleaning products should be used. "Climate control is the most important thing," says Rick. Keep toy robots in a dry room with no radical swings in temperature.

REMINDERS OF SECURITY MEASURES

The photographic employee badges in Rick's collection are an outgrowth of World War I, and they reached a zenith of popularity after World War II began. "They were security measures, which became extremely widespread after England was invaded in World War II," says Rick. "They fascinate me, because we're facing much the same problem [with terrorism] today." Not to be confused with nonphotographic employee badges, war-era photographic employee badges are worth more—from $10 to several hundred dollars. Like any collectible, badges are likely to be found anywhere antiques are sold. Stores, estate sales, and online auctions are Rick's resources.

Deborah and Simon Chasins' COLLECTING INTERESTS span the gamut. Instead of *settling on a single* type of pottery, they invite a RANGE OF VINTAGE wares into their San Diego home, where varied *brands of pottery*—from Bauer and McCoy to RED WING, ROOKWOOD, and Roseville—manage to *coexist beautifully*. As far as this couple is concerned, PEDIGREE AND PRICE make no difference. *Five-dollar* finds, such as the 1930s plates THEY PURCHASED in France,

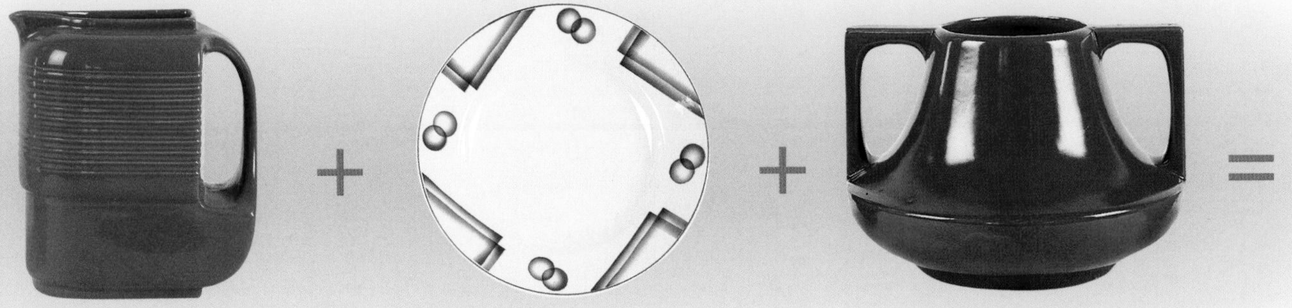

+ ● + =

hold their own alongside rare Clarice Cliff dinnerware from England. Deborah and Simon *collect contemporary* California ART AND FURNITURE, as well as earlier modern classics. The diversity inherent in such a MIXED BAG could look jumbled—but not in this *stylish home,* where color and shape SERVE AS IMPORTANT common denominators that *bring cohesion*. The result in this house: streamlined spaces that are stunning, YET EXTRA EASY on the eye.

All In The Blend

White pottery vases that are approximately the same height and width create what appears to be a uniform display at the living room fireplace. The individual potteries represented include Red Wing, Haeger, Bauer, and Coors.

Playful colors and *shapes* delight the eye in the *living* room.

Start collecting, and you'll begin to see that if you look closely, certain themes appear again and again in decorative arts from different eras, media, and makers. In the Chasins' collections, a Catalina carafe from the 1930s has clean, sculptural lines that make a perfect complement to the couple's modern (1940s and 1950s vintage) and contemporary furniture. Look again: The pottery's bright, solid color echoes the clear palettes of the contemporary paintings the couple enjoys.

A collector with radar for detecting likenesses can make harmony out of diversity. Deborah and Simon are collectors with discerning eyes. Their home is a lesson in making a smooth blend out of a hodgepodge, and they're happy to share their decorating secrets.

As their home shows, the couple looks for similarities in form when mixing collections of different origins.

"I like the graphic nature of the vintage pottery, and how it works with our contemporary furniture and art," says Deborah. "These 1930s pottery pieces show a Deco influence and were considered modern for their time."

The pieces make natural complements for the living room's modern furniture collection, which includes a 1940s Knoll chair and furnishings from the 1950s as well.

Deborah's approach is simple to emulate: She recommends finding your palette and then building collections around colors you love.

"I like a range of color," says Deborah. Thus the Chasins' art, pottery, and furniture all subscribe to a bright palette. Light walls provide essential air around the pieces.

Despite their many different colors, pottery in the Chasins' collection have a similar color value—which means the multicolored pieces can stand together as a unified design statement. Uniform color value (brightness) is a tool for bringing together objects of different hues.

Deborah uses color to mix unlike objects from different collections. In the living room, the modern furniture repeats the gray and green in the pear painting.

Chartreuse-colored

Cubbies bring together pottery of similar shapes and styles—Roseville, Catalina, Bauer, Van Briggle, and Red Wing. Architect John Navalenko designed the chairs and table, which is set with 1938 Manhattan glassware and 1930s French dishware.

Art, furniture, and pottery all share *clean* lines.

1930s Bauer pottery vases reference both furniture and art collections.

The connecting power of color also shows in the home's breakfast area where the golden-yellow tones of the contemporary Asian pear painting are reinforced by the Chinese yellow Bauer pottery. In the guest bedroom, a neutral palette unifies collections of almost rusticated vintage globes, Memphis (a group of postmodern designers) pottery, and contemporary custom furnishings. Without the soothing harmony of color, the three collections otherwise have little in common.

Another of Deborah's strategies is to group disparate objects by color. She loves the clean look of her all-white pottery display on the living room mantel. It doesn't matter that the collection represents four different manufacturers and spans 20 years.

To avoid a cluttered look, these collectors also organized treasures by having niches and shelving built into their home. Floor-to-ceiling cubbies for pottery from all manner of makers and time periods provide a unified front in the dining room. Open shelving in the kitchen is sized to accommodate the collectibles. In other rooms, custom contemporary furniture— yet another collection— incorporates display space into its design.

To maintain an understated look, Deborah and Simon avoid busy patterns in both furnishings and collectibles. Undecorated pottery (with the exception of subtly patterned plates) and furniture upholstered in solid fabrics maintain a serene and simple look.

This home is a lesson in following your instincts when you collect. Deborah's eye rarely errs. She seeks collectibles with similar colors and shapes, which makes the mixing easy.

"There is no snobbery of some objects not being worthy," Deborah explains. "I like those that I bought for $5 as much as the ones that may cost $500."

Now that's a blend.

Open *shelving* is this home's key to a *smooth* blend.

A bold palette of blues, greens, and shades of orange pulls the home together. The chartreuse vases are Bauer except for the tulipiere, which is a 1950s French piece. The pear painting, *The Pilgrimage*, is by San Diego artist Stephen P. Curry.

groupings, clockwise from above left:
Selectively grouping objects without
cluttering surfaces lends elegance to the
overall design of this house. Contemporary
custom furniture by John Navalenko includes
this shelf unit, which displays Memphis
pottery by Michael Duval and world globes
from the 1920s to 1940s that emphasize the
staircase effect. Vintage French dinnerware
echoes patriotic Gallic colors. Vintage
pottery is clustered by similar tones of green.
Uniform shelving allows for subtle color
variation. Bright hues of yellow, green, and
blue animate the kitchen.

A French Accent
On The Table

The French faience dinnerware company, Luneville-St. Clement, is part of Group Sarreguemines, which has been in business since 1728. Different divisions of the group produce different wares: Luneville-St. Clement makes artistic tableware; Digoin makes hotel porcelain, such as the circa-1930s plate shown here from the Chasins' collection. The couple managed to find the Sarreguemines Digoin industrial-style plates for about $1 each at Paris flea markets and at "attic cleanings," which are the French version of garage sales.

Today's Hot Collectible: Refrigerator Ware

When the refrigerator replaced the icebox, appliance makers engaged in at least one marketing scheme that had lasting results: refrigerator ware. The idea was to create serving items that would chill in the fridge without crazing or cracking. This blue water pitcher was made for Westinghouse by the Hall China Company—just one collectible piece among a whole genre of refrigerator ware. Study the distinct Hall colors before you buy; otherwise, you may end up with a piece identical in design but unauthentic in color. Brighten clean pottery with a soft wax, but do not bleach to remove stains, as it weakens the china.

- bluebonnet pottery
- landscape paintings
- texas biedermeier
- horn furniture
- native american weaving
- rosemaled bowls

Place names in the Lone Star State hint of a long, storied past that *inspires collectors* today. Apache Canyon, Neches River, and Comanche County recall *Native American* tribes of the region. San Antonio, Amarillo, Houston, Austin, and many other towns recall Hispanic and *Anglo heritages*. Pore over a map of Texas, and you'll see evidence of the waves of European *immigrants who* settled this promised land in the 1800s.

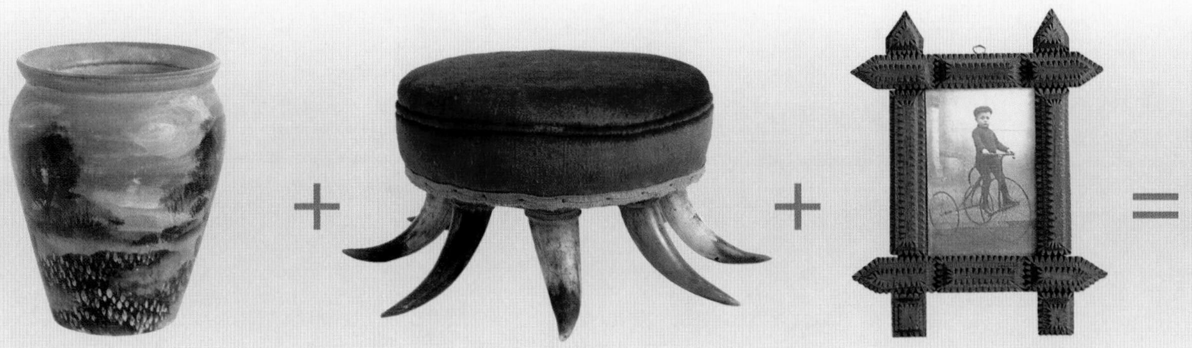

Germans founded Fredericksburg, New Braunfels, and Heidelberg; Nordic settlers honored the Old World with names such as New Swedonia and Stockholm. Dubina, Marak, and New Baden recall *Czech ancestors*. Panna Maria, Texas, claims to be the oldest permanent Polish settlement in America. In a single Houston farmhouse, native Texan and antiques dealer Harold Hollis *gathers collectibles* from all these cultures.

A Texan's Roundup

Bluebonnets, the official state flower, are dear to Texans' hearts. The flower lends its name to cheerful souvenir pottery manufactured before 1950. Antiques dealer Harold Hollis displays some of his pieces in a wall cupboard.

Harold Hollis' white clapboard house, sitting unassumingly near one of Houston's busiest intersections, is a reminder of past agricultural days. The modest 19th-century structure brims with Texas history. Surprisingly, Harold discovered after buying the house that his great-grandfather owned it many years before.

The collection Hollis has amassed reflects the Lone Star State's multicultural heritage. "I have Anglo things, Texas-German, Texas-Polish, Texas-Czech, and even Spanish pieces," he says. "That's one of the nifty things about collecting in a part of the world where there are so many cultures: You get all this variety."

Texas beauties jam the dealer's three-bedroom home, creating an easygoing—rather than cluttered—atmosphere that invites you to amble through and enjoy. Vintage landscapes of bluebonnets enliven the moss green walls, pottery fills shelves, and hooked rugs and Native American weavings cover beds and chairs.

Thanks to designer Ralph Lauren, furniture made of cowhide and cow horns, fading photographs of cowboys, and Southwestern basketry may have made their statement in today's popular culture; but Harold, a purist at heart, says he prefers the true Texas collectibles as opposed to a line of wares that come and go with fickle fashion.

He doesn't mind a setting that's a bit rough around the edges. After buying his house, Harold revitalized the pine floors by buffing them. But perfection is not a hangup. He likes the notion that there is a phantom hint of the linoleum floors that a previous owner had used to cover the pine. Harold wishes that the fellow had not freshened the age-darkened pine wainscoting. "I would have left it the way it was," he says. "Only time can achieve that color."

"Old houses come with problems," says Harold, who does without modern conveniences, such as fuel-saving insulation. "But I like living in them; they're suited to the kinds of things that I collect."

"Collecting in a part of the *world* where there are so many *cultures*—you get variety."

A German-speaking immigrant translated the lines of simple, well-proportioned mid-19th-century Biedermeier into this sofa. The artisan used woods native to Texas—a contrast to the more refined blond pieces typically made in Europe.

above: Harold discovered this locally made horn bench in Tombale, near Houston. The bed is made of mesquite, a native wood that lends distinctive flavor to barbecue but was rarely used in making furniture. **right:** Inherited from an aunt, a cabinet houses Texas centennial glasses, Texas pharmacy bottles, and Staffordshire commemorating campaigns from the Mexican-American War. **left:** A vintage collectible, this 1947 Chambers range is a hot kitchen showpiece. **far left:** Valued rugs, such as the folk art hooked rug, hang safely on the wall.

Texas Bluebonnets Bloom On

Hand-painted bluebonnet pottery was manufactured as souvenir pieces in San Antonio by the firm Meyer in the first half of the 20th century. This line of generally small, bright pieces—including jugs, bowls, and toothpick holders—answered the demand for inexpensive souvenirs during the Texas Centennial in Dallas. Today, the ceramics, rarely marked, fetch handsome prices, depending on their size and condition. Meyer also manufactured much of the large, unembellished, mellow-tone crockery that Harold collects. The Round Top Antiques Fair, held in central Texas, is a hot spot for collecting bluebonnet pottery. Round Top, the tiniest incorporated town in Texas, multiplies its population by thousands twice each year when collectors from every state and abroad flock there to shop.

Furniture Romances The Frontier

By the late 19th century, craftsmen captured the spirit of the Old West and its cattle days by creating hat racks, chairs, and other pieces, such as this ottoman, from the horns of Texas longhorn cattle. Horn furniture appeared at exhibitions and state fairs, and also was sold in the East and exported to Europe. Wenzel Friedrich, a cabinetmaker from Bohemia, settled in San Antonio and made some of the most original pieces. He counted among his clients Queen Victoria, Otto von Bismarck, and Kaiser Wilhelm I. Horn furniture also flourished from the 1930s to the 1950s, the heyday of cowboy pictures and rustic style.

metal banks

vintage glass

action figures

matchbooks

state plates

swizzle sticks

Molly and Leon Banowetz of EAST DALLAS, TEXAS, have an *eye-popping* good time, surrounded as they are by a disparate array of objects, from STATE PLATES and vintage glass to crucifixes *and cue balls.* Their collection of globes—actually metal banks SHOWING HOW countries' BORDERS HAVE changed over the years—seems an appropriate symbol for these *graphic designers:* They creatively *push boundaries.* On purchasing their 3,000-

+ + =

square-foot COLONIAL-STYLE HOME, the Banowetzes could have safely *decorated with* Chippendale- and Federal-style pieces. Instead, they *charged fearlessly* ahead, TRANSCENDING THE CONFINES of restrained architecture by playing up their *offbeat collections* and funky furnishings. Friends must delight in the COCKTAIL HOUR, especially with Molly's *swizzle sticks* from all over the world as PART OF THE setting. Here's to unpredictability!

COOL KITSCH RULES

Small item collections have more visual impact when grouped together, as shown by these crucifixes and candles. The intricate beauty of the stair rail, an antiques road trip find, came to light after layers of paint were stripped away.

Molly and Leon Banowetz are crazy for collections—the kitschier, the better: metal globes that function as banks, old swizzle sticks, glassware bocci balls, souvenir state plates, matchbooks, crosses, toy whistles, and much more.

Such an amalgam might have overwhelmed

A simple color scheme serves as a backdrop for varied collections.

their East Dallas, Texas, home. "We had everything, all the collections, in boxes when we moved in," says Leon. "We just didn't know what to do with them."

As the first chore on the list, they calmed the patchwork of different paint colors in the house—royal blues and hunter greens. The Banowetzes coated every room in a creamy vanilla and freshened most of the trim with a glistening white enamel. "If you keep the color scheme simple, it makes the stuff in the room a lot more interesting," says Leon.

Then the couple opened up the house by adding an off-the-kitchen deck and replacing windows in the dining room and the kitchen with French doors. "They give us light and access to the deck for entertaining," says Leon.

With a calm backdrop in place, the Banowetzes were ready to cut loose. To stash their collections in a smart way, they called on Kelly O'Neal, a designer and partner in the Dallas interiors store, Legacy Trading Co.

Kelly and an associate excitedly tore through the boxes of collectibles. "He was like a kid at Christmas," says Leon.

Kelly transformed the house in one day by opting to use what his client had on hand. His presentations gave the collections a new twist. "Kelly moved items around," says Leon. "He

did things with our stuff that we never would have thought of."

Controlled chaos sums up Kelly's strategy for handling these engaging, yet unorthodox, belongings. One of his recommended solutions is grouping like objects, which is easily done with shelves.

He also believes small items have more impact grouped together than when spread about. For example, Molly's grouping of delicate crucifixes complements the lines of the graceful banister, which the Banowetzes "dipped and stripped" of many coats of paint before uncovering its brass accents.

Bookcases *transformed* into glass-front display cases protect *breakables*.

Built-in cabinets, which are coated in glistening white enamel, frame the entrance to a cocktail room. The exposed wall is painted an ocean of indigo, with the framed matchbook collection functioning as an artistic focal point.

left: The dining room table was stripped down to basics and repainted. Glass replaced its ornate top. right: Souvenir state plates and cue balls, serving as accessories, keep the ho-hum out of entertaining. No doubt the conversation is brisk and lively in this setting.

The designer also edits furniture. "You get used to seeing things together," he says. "Just because you have it does not mean you have to use it." Kelly infused the living room with fresh energy by pairing red California contemporary chairs with the traditionally styled cut-velvet sofa. Painted storage trunks were converted into side tables for another interesting and lively touch.

Kelly suggested changing the open bookcases into glass-front display cabinets to keep collections in order and to protect breakables. A myriad of glassware—in all shapes, sizes, and colors—lines the shelves. In this mix, Molly's swizzle sticks find a home in souvenir glasses.

Action figures that originally belonged to a nephew crowd a cupboard. These collectibles are great fun for adults who haven't outgrown their childhood heroes, such as GI Joe, Batman, Superman, and Spiderman. Other collectible figures include Ninja Turtles, Power Rangers, X-Men, and characters from *Star Wars* and *Star Trek*.

White cabinets surround the entrance to a "cocktail room," where Kelly had the exposed wall painted an ocean of indigo. This color block functions as an eye-stopping canvas for Leon's framed collection of matchbooks, which functions as witty contemporary art.

The designer avoids pattern, which "becomes dated quicker than anything. Color as an accent always stays in."

Sometimes it's possible to create order by starting from the bottom up. "A good rug can bring a room together," notes Kelly. A red rug—an amazing yard sale find—serves as another color block, anchoring the area in front of the cocktail room. The Banowetzes paired the rug with simple antiques.

Innovative color and furnishings, as well as strategic use of shelf and wall space, make these fun collections cool, never campy.

above: Molly designed the bed and commissioned metal artisans to execute it. The sun represents her husband's tendency to wake up early, while the moon symbolizes her habit of rising late. **right:** Leon is partial to matchbooks because they're colorful reminders of special moments and events. **left:** Action figures, originally belonging to a nephew, pack a visual punch when loaded on shelves. **far left:** Molly began amassing swizzle sticks when she bought a cigar box full for $10.

Let Your Glassware Sparkle And Shine

Glassware, whether antique or contemporary, deserves tender loving care. Here's the secret to cleaning it—without damaging the surface. Before you begin, remove any rings and bracelets so you won't cause scratches. Pad your sink with a cotton towel; then wash your pieces by hand in cool, never more than tepid, water. Aggressive chemicals may stain or discolor glass, so use a liquid hand-washing soap low in alkaline. Some curators advocate a strong solution of baking soda. Immerse one piece at a time, gently rubbing with a cotton cloth; then rinse in a solution of tepid water and a capful of vinegar. Rinse thoroughly again by showering the piece with the spray attachment of your sink. To prevent streaks, dry your glassware with a soft cotton towel.

Happy Travels: State Plates

Baby boomers remember summer road trips when parents, brothers, and sisters piled in station wagons to explore the diverse regions of the United States. Visiting every state in the country was the goal, often accomplished over several summers. Families documented their tours by choosing inexpensive souvenirs at tourist shops. Today people tend to zip down interstates. Those nostalgic for easygoing vacations collect state plates, spoons, snow globes, and other memorabilia.

Chapter 3

What do YOUR COLLECTIONS say about you? It's all in the editing. Before writing a paragraph, you *have to decide* what you want your words to say; THE SAME IS TRUE when *choosing and* displaying your collections. Before you can put a room or a display together, YOU SHOULD HAVE a message in mind. *Choose objects* that tell your personal story, then create arrangements that lead the eye to pieces

EDITING YOUR
Collections

that *deserve notice*. These editing tips can get you going:
● DISCIPLINE YOURSELF. Don't feel you must display everything you love at once. Put a *few things* away for a while so THE TREASURES that remain can get all due notice. Then *rotate your* collections as the mood strikes.
● Leave BREATHING ROOM. Like a mat around an art print, blank space *highlights* objects on a wall, tabletop, or shelf.

japanese ikebana baskets

architectural fragments

looking glasses

southern antiques

architectural drawings

windsor chairs

Beaufort, South Carolina, on PORT ROYAL ISLAND, looking out *over the waters* of its namesake river and the islands beyond, is a GENTEEL COASTAL LADY. As with so many *Southern locales*, this town, established in 1711, is imbued with a strong SENSE OF HISTORY. Hernando de Soto marched *through the area* as far back as 1520, and early capture by United States troops SPARED BEAUFORT'S architecture *the ravages of* the Civil War. The 18th- and

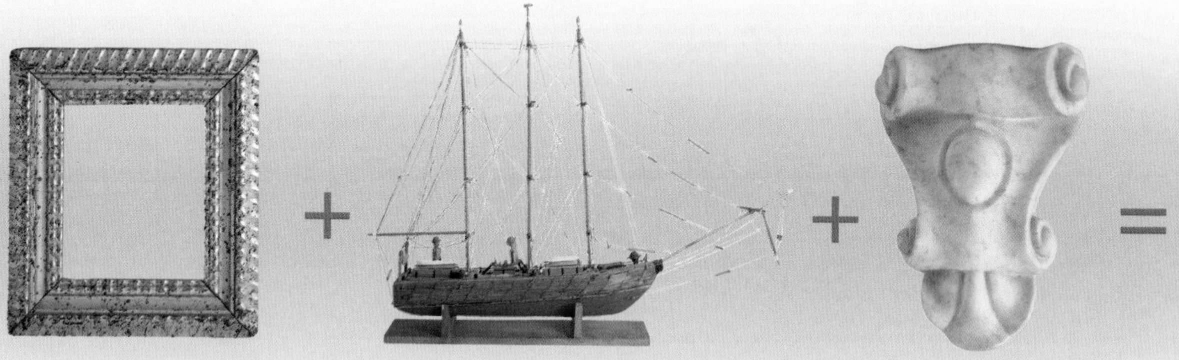

19th-century American PIECES gracing the 1790 house owned by Michael Rainey echo, in placement, *the classical* RESTRAINT TYPICAL of the Federal period. Michael is not a purist; after all, he is a Marine Corps *fighter pilot turned dealer*. He also ACCENTS HIS COLLECTION with prizes that he discovered *while traveling* in Italy and Japan. ARCHITECTURAL FRAGMENTS and Japanese baskets *coexist harmoniously* with his American pieces.

SOUTHERN REFINED

A trio of frames makes an intriguing composition in the living room. The circa-1800 secretary is crafted of cherry with mahogany banding; scallop molding softens its linear style. The prim Windsor chair dates from the 1700s.

Michael disdains the notion of a museumlike setting, although curators probably wouldn't mind acquiring some of his high-quality furnishings from New England, Pennsylvania, and the South. Along with beauty, his house exists for comfort, as his upholstered furnishings, which are his only nonantiques, attest.

"I knew I didn't want to create a museum atmosphere, but a place that was fun to live in," Michael says.

Symmetry, fundamentally when one element balances another, is a hallmark of 18th-century neoclassic design and dominates the living room. A pair of unadorned windows on each side of the fireplace allows natural light to wash in.

Michael, however, did not refrain from experimenting in a house with bones this old. All the mantels in the house had been sold, so he used door surrounds from a derelict building around the fireplace. The lines of the mantel suggest fluted Ionic and Doric columns, with a fan motif at center.

"I was just sitting around one evening in front of the fireplace, and I started wondering what the fireplace surround would look like painted red," he says. The color dramatically plays up a period marble bust of Napoleon, which resides in the fireplace during warm months. The mantel serves as an ideal resting place for a cluster of objets d'art, from Italian marble architectural remnants to a small-size American Impressionist painting.

On each side of the room's fireplace, cast-iron garden urns filled with liriope lend a casual air. "I'm not much for raising houseplants," he says, "but I thought, with all the dark antiques, the room needed a little color." He grows his own orchids in a nearby greenhouse.

In the living room, the dealer also deftly uses asymmetry, another important 18th-century aesthetic in which balance is accomplished by using unequal elements. For example, Michael places three looking glasses—Chippendale, Sheraton (with gold leaf and

"I knew I didn't want to create a *museum atmosphere*, but a place that was fun to live in."

A period bust of Napoleon, who fell from emperor's grace, commands attention from the fireplace. The mantel is a testament to owner Michael Rainey's ingenuity: He used door surrounds from a derelict building to create it.

"Really good *Southern* pieces are hard to find, and they're very *expensive.*"

The kitchen, lovely in its spare approach, showcases Ikebana baskets, which are used in Japanese flower arranging. The modest shelves are meant to support, never distract. This Asian sensibility melds with fine Southern pieces.

ebonized twists), and Queen Anne—next to the window on the right, whereas a single slightly larger Chippendale mirror hangs next to the window on the left.

He counts the mirrors among his favorite collections. "They range in style from Queen Anne to Sheraton, from 1740 to 1810," he says. "All have their original surface, all have their original glass, and all have a nice dark color. They're really not very functional."

Again, Michael asserts his light decorating touch by placing custom-made club chairs, comfy and sensible, on either side of a circa-1800 child's drop-leaf cherry table. A more predictable homeowner would have made do with a coffee table.

The kitchen, though less formal, represents a trove of fine antiques. For instance, a Virginia raised-panel hanging cupboard dates from the 1860s. Japanese Ikebana baskets are poised delicately above a solid Alabama sugar chest. Sugar was once a precious commodity on the frontier edges of the early republic as Americans pushed west beyond the original 13

colonies. The settlers locked up their sugar, which was not granulated but rather in a loaf form wrapped in paper. Special nippers were used to break off a piece of this sweet pioneer luxury.

Windsor chairs make for charmed seating at breakfast. The early Georgia table, circa 1800, is something to feast your eyes upon: It still sports the original red paint, which contributes to its value—and charm.

Michael travels enough to keep up his voracious appetite as a collector and dealer. To complement the style of his Federal house, he avoids clutter.

"I've tried to add one or two good pieces each year, but now the house is kind of full," he says. "That's why I went into the antiques business—to stay involved."

Michael shares the joy of the hunt, as well as his good taste and knowledge, with others. Any client who frequents his house will learn an immediate lesson on balancing collections to their best advantage.

above: In the vibrant, blue-green library, Michael mixes miniatures, more than 100 snuffboxes, and rare decoys among books. below: Eccentricity crowns the serious, with antique puppet heads atop a 1790 Chippendale chest.

clockwise from top: Michael thematically places together objects, such as nautical antiques, including a pond sailer with a lead keel and a military uniform and swords. English and American snuffboxes, dating from 1740 to 1820, have visual impact en masse. A Southern gentleman's house would seem incomplete without a collection of antique walking canes. Marble Italian architectural fragments enhance the living room mantel. The lines of this circa-1760 Queen Anne birch chest from Connecticut anticipate the later Chippendale style.

"A Thing Of Beauty Is A Joy Forever"

John Keats wrote these immortal words almost 200 years ago, yet how relevant they are today, given the popularity of architectural fragments, as in this small piece of Italian marble. The simple "S" curve and the suggestion of a shell motif are much-appreciated classical elements. In the last decade, the quest for remnants of the past has intensified. Bits of old buildings find new life as ornaments on indoor surfaces and in outdoor rooms. Homeowners freely exert their decorating flair in repurposing larger items—gates, doors, cast-iron benches, gargoyles, mantels, ecclesiastical furnishings, pillars, statuary, urns, fountains, and fences.

Swept Away By Nautical Themes

This 19th-century pond sailer conjures up images of children launching model ships in the pools of public gardens. If the sea lures you on a small scale, drop by the United States Naval Academy Museum in Annapolis, Maryland, to study the finest ship models from the 17th, 18th, and 19th centuries. Nautical antiques are fresh accents in lake or ocean houses, in offices, or in children's rooms. Use ship's clocks and bells, barometers, life rings, signal flags, sextants, telescopes, compasses, or maritime paintings—and let your imagination set sail.

People seek to SIMPLIFY THEIR LIVES, probably in reaction to the stepped-up pace of *modern-day life*. Chicago design PARTNERS Anne Kaplan and Bruce Goers took on a challenge when they *assisted a family* in downsizing from a 10,000-square-foot LAKESIDE MANSION to a 3,500-square-foot *brick townhouse*. For a typical family of three, such a move might BE FAIRLY ORDINARY, but these clients *were different:* They had become accustomed to

spreading out over their large home—along with their collections of ANCIENT AND MODERN works gathered for more *than 30 years*. Most of their pieces are by Native Americans from NORTH AND SOUTH AMERICA. When space gets cut by almost two-thirds, *designers must be* innovative. ANNE AND BRUCE, striving to fit in every possible object, *used color* to defeat the banality of MUSEUMLIKE WHITE WALLS and rethought use of space.

MINIMAL ARTIFACTS

"Ancient meets modern" is the recurring theme in this townhouse. A 20-foot-tall Pacific Northwest totem pole and a smaller carved pole flank the fireplace, which has a black marble mantel and a blue steel fireplace surround.

In downsizing from roomy quarters to a townhouse, the owners wanted to meld their collection of ancient artifacts with their thoroughly modern lifestyle. The last thing they desired was an institutional setting.

"The house had wonderful height and no dimension," says Bruce Goers. "All the walls were painted white. With all the artwork, we didn't want the place to look like a museum."

With partner Anne Kaplan, Bruce put colors and angles to pleasing use. For instance, six colors—ranging from lavender, green, and burnt orange—delineate the living room. To define the boxiness of the entrance, the designers papered the area around the front door with sheets of barkcloth, then, for contrast, painted the stair railing bronze.

Thoughtfully placed objects fascinate visitors, drawing them into a setting that forces a new perspective on centuries-old objects. Lavender walls offer a soft contrast to ancient sculptures, which hold a prominent place atop a primitive Iowa cupboard. Rugs sporting geometric patterns subtly dazzle, as does an antique table displaying pre-Columbian pipe sculptures.

The eye-stopper in the living room is a 20-foot totem pole, a fixture in the owners' previous yard. Unlike totem poles with serious expressions, this one puts on a series of happy faces.

The owners' furniture also presented some design challenges. Large pieces and smaller room dimensions did not go together until the designers reassigned spaces. In turning the family room into a dining room, they managed to squeeze in a 13-foot-long antique English table. They also transformed the original dining room into a media room with four reclining chairs and on oversize ottoman.

Seemingly incongruous pieces, when given enough space, can coexist. Perhaps the most interesting juxtaposition is the outrageous contemporary Italian seating amid serious artifacts. But such a contrast expresses how comfortably this family lives with its art.

Seemingly incongruous pieces—when given enough space—*comfortably* coexist.

Here is a daring decorative mix: primitive masks, a totem pole, and Italian seating with swivel head-, arm-, and footrests and attached rotating tables. For even more texture, raffia cloth covers the wall behind the bookcase shelves.

above: Bowls, baskets, and raffia decoratively connect the functional kitchen to the rest of the house. **left:** Sheer curtains soften the dining room. On the overmantel are Narino ceremonial bowls from the border region between Colombia and Ecuador. They date from the 6th through 12th centuries. **right:** The antique English dining table and modern office chairs make an unusual pairing. An early 1900s Plains tribe tepee liner hangs above two 19th-century Japanese tansu chests, raised to buffet height on an iron stand.

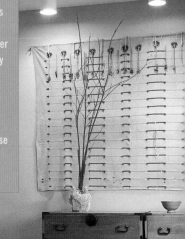

Native American Textiles Dazzle

Vintage and antique Native American textiles have long been prized for their patterns, colors, and historic merit. Contemporary textiles also have great appeal, and their prices are within reach of more collectors. Anyone curious about such textiles can gain knowledge by visiting museums and established dealers. *American Indian Textiles: 2,000 Artist Biographies* (2001) by Gregory Schaff, Ph.D., profiles more than 1,000 textiles from the past 200 years by Navajo rug weavers, as well as textile artists representing Hopi, Zuni, Rio Grand Pueblo, Cherokee, Osage, and other Native American peoples.

Ancient Beauty Lives Today

Today, objects dating from the pre-Columbian and colonial periods are not easily exported from most countries in Central and South America. In fact, such pieces can be declared property of most of these countries, which do not readily grant government permission for their export. It is possible, however, to collect quality pieces produced by contemporary craftspeople. Fine shops, as well as museums, offer replicas that capture the distinctive aesthetics of indigenous peoples. Log on to www.TribalArtsDirectory.com to learn more about Native American art.

One hundred years ago, AMERICAN AND EUROPEAN *audiences thrilled* to the daring performances of Harry Houdini, history's most CELEBRATED MAGICIAN. He *could slip from* any restraint—handcuffs, jail cells, straitjackets, and coffins. The ESCAPE ARTIST still intrigues *admirers today,* including Dom DiMento, whose home overlooks SAN FRANCISCO BAY. This collector's life *was transformed* 20 years ago when he

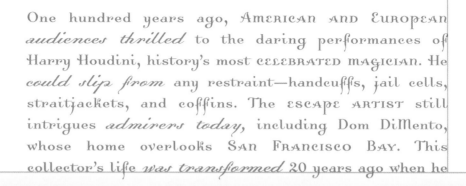

bought a lithographed theatrical *poster of a magician,* which cast a LASTING SPELL. Dom began accumulating posters, as well as programs, *photographs,* periodicals, letters, and other objects, from the GOLDEN AGE of magic, which lasted *from the mid-19th* century until the 1920s. Despite his extensive collection, Dom MANAGES to select and *display objects* throughout his house— as deftly as a magician PULLING A RABBIT out of a hat.

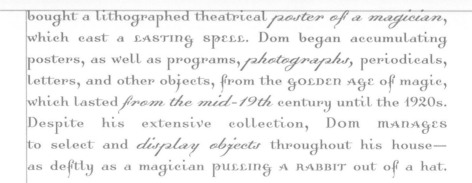

A MAGICAL ESCAPE

A sitting area in the kitchen makes a great place to display parts of the collection, including a wonderful 1920s French Pierrot mannequin in a child's costume and a cleverly animated poster of the magician Roody.

A circa-1920 poster of illusionist Horace Goldin is an entertaining piece. Goldin, in the white suit, claimed to have originated the trick of sawing a woman in half and also gained renown for supposedly making a tiger disappear.

Less than two years after the purchase of his first theatrical poster, Dom's collection outgrew the San Francisco apartment he shared with Craig Lyall. They moved across the Bay Bridge to a 1927 California Mediterranean-style house. The two-story stucco needed remodeling—a project that offered a chance to create precious display space for collectibles.

Dom's visual acuity as a graphic designer contributed to the success of this undertaking. Above the kitchen, he and Craig added a library and storage area, which they made accessible by opening a cramped downstairs hallway. This arched pass-through now functions as a gallery space for Dom's posters.

The house's lighting is aimed at illuminating the collection. Dom himself installed central lighting and recessed low-wattage halogen lights for display.

His lithographed theatrical posters deserve the spotlight. The heyday of magic performances coincided with technical excellence in lithography, which was executed by mostly anonymous staff artists in print shops.

Some of Dom's favorite works are by the magician known simply as "Kellar." He used exquisite paper and fantastical designs. Strobridge Printing Company in Cincinnati, Ohio—considered the Tiffany of lithographers—printed the material.

Dom's collections of magic objects are so extensive that he must choose what comes out of storage. "In a museum, some pieces have to go up to tell the full story," he says. "Your home display does not have that obligation. In a home, the furniture, rugs, and so forth reflect who you are. So should the choices of your collection."

The colorful collections play nicely against the background of subtle walls and against the simple linear furnishings, such as Mission. Rugs throughout the house, many warmed with red tones, enrich the setting, as do Dom's 2,000 books—which are either instruction in the "mystic art" or histories of magic and its practitioners. The

"**Furniture and rugs** *reflect* **who you are. So should your choices of** *collections.*"

majority are Victorian and have intricately embossed covers. Dom looks for volumes in good condition, with richly produced covers, whether the content is significant or not. He also will purchase a pamphlet if it has historical value, even though the piece may not be graphically appealing.

This house pulls off the trick desired by every homeowner—to delight and enchant. Certainly, Houdini and Kellar would be pleased.

99

above left: Dom considers Kellar's posters to exemplify the best in magic graphic arts.
above: Dom built and designed the cherry bed in the master bedroom. Its simple aesthetic complements other furnishings in the house.
right: This automated conjurer with a velvet-skirted table does a cups-and-ball trick. Leopold Lambert manufactured it in France about 1890. **left:** This grandly sized 1895 Harry Houdini—a stellar piece in Dom's collection—greets visitors. The famed magician strikes what is known as the "Harry for President" pose.

Protect Precious Works On Paper

Keep paper collectibles away from temperature extremes, excessive light, and uneven humidity levels. Framed documents or works of art on paper are best preserved if professionally hinged into mats that have both a backboard and a window board. Make sure your picture framer uses museum-quality, or acid-free, mat board. Otherwise, mat burn, or dark yellow staining around the edges of the window mat, will occur and discolor the art. Use frames with mitered joints. A window mat or spacer is necessary to prevent contact with glass.

Games: More Than Child's Play

Children's magic sets represent just one type of collectible affiliated with games and other amusements. Don't toy with an antique or vintage game, which ideally belongs undisturbed in its box. Always don gloves, just as a museum curator would when handling a bronze sculpture, a piece of furniture, or any other artifact. This protective measure will keep oil on your hands—which causes deterioration—from coming into contact with the object. Pick up the box with both hands, exerting no pressure on the top. If you find it necessary to get into a game, open it from both sides simultaneously.

- heywood-wakefield
- glass paperweights
- 1950s italian glass
- eames furniture
- wedgwood pottery
- barbecue trays

Like *their 1955 home* in the Midwest, Joan and Gary Gand are children of the 1950s. THEY'RE ALSO DESIGN purists who *make no apologies* for thinking inside the box. The only decorating style that's an *aesthetic* soul mate for THEIR HOUSE, they insist, is 1950s modern—furnishings and *art objects* cut from the same mold as the architecture. A HARD-LINE APPROACH? You bet. *The Gands'* 1950s Knoll and Eames sofas feature one

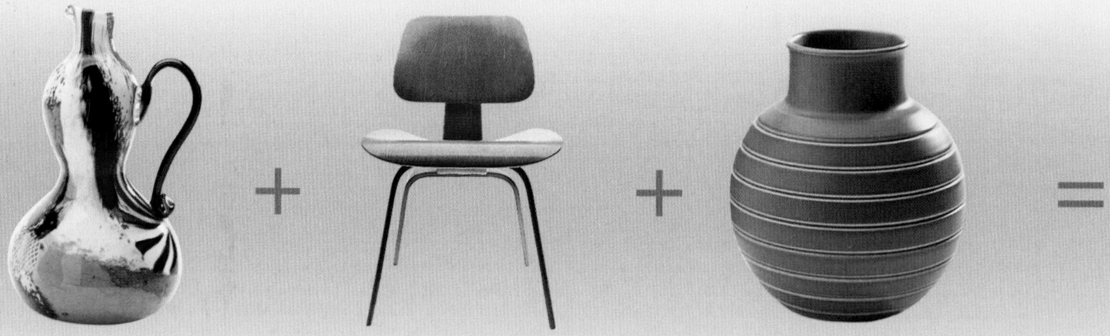

SHARP ANGLE after another. Other classics from the era—the fluid shapes of *furniture pieces* by Aalvar Aalto and HEYWOOD-WAKEFIELD—soften the scene. Splashy 1950s *Italian glassware* brightens the blond WOODS AND CHROME, but displays are kept strictly in order. The sinewy, *patchwork-colored* glass is COMPARTMENTALIZED—one wall for this maker, another FOR THAT. Not even *June Cleaver* ran a tighter ship.

Focus On The Fifties

A Heywood-Wakefield sofa and a glass-topped coffee table in the style of Noguchi anchor the sunroom. Freestanding shelves display Keith Murray-designed Wedgwood pottery on the left and American studio pottery on the right.

"Finding the right *furniture* and accessories was like putting together the pieces of a *puzzle*."

Space-age shapes and materials pull together the furniture collection, which includes a black leather and chrome Eames Sofa Compact and the Warren Platner wire and glass coffee and end tables by Knoll.

The Gands achieve an edited look, even with an abundance of objects. Vividly colored Italian glassware spills over shelves and tabletops, and swells into the hundreds. Wares from specific manufacturers, such as Barovier and Venini, constitute collections in their own right. So why the clean look? Focus, focus, focus.

Their collections are limited to the 1950s, with a little fudging on either side of the decade. Reining in furniture, art, and accessories to a limited time frame gives rooms a homogeneous look. When the architecture is from the same era, the focus sharpens. With nothing helter-skelter to confuse the eye, even large quantities of collectibles nestle in visual peace.

The couple continues the clean design by editing furniture to a few stellar 1950s pieces. Quality, not quantity, makes the collection strong. Even the furniture arrangement tightens the focus. "We collected a lot of period books with the original photographs to get a sense of what the decorating trends were at the time," says Gary.

A simpatico relationship between the architecture and furniture gives the living room a "low, long look," says Joan. Because of its streamlined form, most modern furniture (not just 1950s vintage) has a head start over other collectibles in achieving an uncluttered look. When furniture and architecture create a crisp, graphic backdrop, it's easier to fill the edges with other collectibles with no danger of appearing unkempt.

True to the period as a 50-year flashback, the architecture and furniture stick to a monochromatic palette of quiet neutrals. When a simplified look is the goal, a hushed, pattern-free palette proves valuable.

In contrast to the understated furnishings, the Italian glassware is robust with tension and multifarious hues. Such a mix of colors and shapes, especially in these quantities, could be confusing. Here, however, chaos is chastened by floating the collection along glass shelving against a gallery-white wall. Despite its numbers, the display is disciplined—three pieces

Aluminum group Eames chairs join an Aalvar Aalto coffee table in the bedroom. The bookcase contains pottery by Eugene Deutch, French glass paperweights, and Italian glass vases, including a Christine Diro signature vase by Barovier.

per shelf usually. Museumlike organization has one wall featuring only glassware from Italy's preeminent Venini company; the other displays designs by artist Dino Martens.

Odds-and-ends pieces are corralled in the bedroom. A classification system prevails, with one wall of shelving showcasing exclusively Barovier glassware. "We try not to mix the Barovier with other pieces because its colors and shapes are different," says Gary. Elsewhere in the room, there's more freedom to mix—but with no disruption of serenity. Like stones in a Zen garden, each piece feels

so carefully chosen and placed as to be inevitable. Gary suggests even this is a 1950s thing: "I remember my mom having a decorator talk to her about colors and the placement of things in a room according to space and geometry," says Gary. "Now we call it feng shui."

Pottery replaces glassware in the sunroom. The two featured collections include pottery designed in the mid-1930s by architect Keith Murray for Wedgwood and American studio pottery similar in feel to Murray's Wedgwood, but handmade by various studio artisans from the

late 1940s through the 1950s. To avoid confusion, all the Wedgwood is on one side of the room and all the American studio on the other. Combined with the curvaceous shapes and blond wood of the Heywood-Wakefield furniture, the muted-colored pottery adds to the room's organic feel.

The kitchen is the place for kitsch—and fun. Barbecue trays, 1950s cookbooks, Fiesta dinnerware, and George Nelson clocks make the space pulsate with energy. All that's missing, says Gary, is a skillet-wielding housewife in an apron.

above: Aalvar Aalto barstools and an Italian table extend the 1950s furniture collection to the kitchen. The table's centerpiece is a Barovier Intarsio patchwork vase from the early 1960s. Flowers casually grace a green Aalvar Aalto Savoy vase. **far left:** Italian glassware features bright, beautiful color blocks. **left:** The kitchen collection includes barbecue trays and Fiesta, Mettlox California Freeform, Hall, Red Wing, and Franciscan Starburst pottery. **right:** French glass paperweights sporting intricate designs form yet another collection.

What's In A Name?
Value, If It's Venini

Originally intrigued by Venini glassware they saw at auctions, Gary and Joan hit their decorating and collecting books to learn all they could. They decided that brightly colored modern Italian glass was the "ultimate art object for this house," says Joan. It also represented the ultimate commitment—"like deciding to have kids. But we both wanted to do it, so we jumped in with both feet," says Gary. A passion was born. Now experts, they can tell a vintage Venini—the most famous of the Venetian glass companies, and still in business—at a glance. Furthermore, they can tell you that the Venini shown here was designed by Fulvio Bianconi, and that the colors and fluid shapes mean its style is Pezzato. Their best advice for those who want to begin a collection: Look and learn before buying, and start saving money. This collectible can be pricey.

The Barbecue Basics

Like most collections, the Gands' 1950s pieces started out humbly. They didn't have the luxury of investing for looks only; their collectibles needed to function, which is why 1950s kitchen collectibles were perfect. "I love to barbecue, so we started collecting barbecue trays," says Gary. The tomato red trays brighten the room, and they're still performing a service, even though the Gands' budget no longer demands function from their collections. The graphics on the tray were designed by a Chicago architect and illustrator named Stoyke; surprisingly, at least for the 1950s, she was a woman.

Hollywood's FIRST "REEL" MEN—cowboys who rode tall in their celluloid saddles—*captivated hordes* of children, as well as their parents. Tom Mix, the squeaky-clean hero astride Tony the Wonder Horse, was *the top wrangler* of the silent-film era. Hoot Gibson, the stuntman turned *comedic cowboy*, drew cheers from audiences. A generation later, Gene Autry, with his TRADEMARK SONG "Back in the Saddle Again," *yodeled his way* into

American hearts with HIT MOVIES AND RECORDS. Though inaccurately depicted on the *silver screen*, images of the Old West spawned nostalgia for RUGGED WESTERN interiors and Hispanic influences between the World Wars. *Today this* period inspires Neil Korpenin and interior design partner Erik Erikson, who REFURBISHED their 1930s *rancho-style* Palm Springs, California, home, using collectibles to give it an *appropriately Western* twang.

CALIFORNIA RUSTIC

Monterey furnishings are a prized collection; the style is unique to the California Arts and Crafts tradition from the 1920s until the 1940s. The wagon-wheel base of the chandelier complements the scale of the table and sideboard.

"Monterey *furniture* was based on a chair that was in an old *Cisco Kid* movie."

Earthy tones, rough texture, and exposed beams are reminiscent of the Old West conjured up by Hollywood. Textiles feature Mexican patterns, such as bright stripes, and Native American influences, such as jagged lines and diamonds.

Neil Korpenin was on a mission: to find the perfect sofa for his house in the desert. He had to dig for the treasure—in this case a Monterey sofa—obscured by cast-aside couches, beat-up sideboards, chairs with broken arms and legs, and packing blankets in a Los Angeles warehouse. He immediately saw the piece's character, despite springs punching through the cushions. The spindles were serpentine and the arms as wide and flat as boat oars.

"It was rustic—the kind of furniture cowboys would have, if cowboys had furniture," says Neil.

Then the hunt was on. He and Erik Erikson scoured southwestern California for pieces of Monterey. The furniture, produced by the Mason Manufacturing Company in Los Angeles from the 1920s until the 1940s, was unique to the California Arts and Crafts tradition.

"The furniture was based on a chair that was in an old Cisco Kid movie," says Neil. "A designer who saw the movie put together a line of furniture based on the chair for a California department store, and they called it Monterey."

The furniture's generous proportions and sturdiness somehow harken back to the West's immense open spaces.

"Monterey is utilitarian," says Neil. "Look at the arms on the chairs. They're wide enough to hold a plate."

In the first few years of production, Mason manufactured 120 different pieces: 3 bedroom sets, 6 dining room sets, 16 upholstery pieces, 16 occasional and coffee tables, and 4 desks and secretaries.

About the time Monterey became vogue, Palm Springs was becoming a Hollywood hot-spot retreat. Neil and Erik's 1930s rancho-style house is a spacious backdrop for their Western collectibles. Typical of the architectural style of the period, each room has its own set of double doors that lead to garden areas. The three bedrooms and kitchen all open onto the dramatic living room.

Unfortunately, previous owners had diminished its sense of space. Wall-to-wall carpet smothered a cement floor, originally stained and incised into grids to resemble clay tiles. A 1960s shade of aqua coated almost everything. A mansard-style mantelpiece disguised the rugged stone fireplace.

Neil and Erik stripped away decades of such inappropriate decorating. The house, rugged and spacious once more, is an artful blend of California Arts and Crafts ambience and the Southwest ranch style of the mid-1800s, with its low-slung profile and tile roof.

Is there room for more Monterey? Maybe—but the pieces are tougher to find, and the prices of these once thrift-market finds have skyrocketed. Meanwhile, this designer duo will happily settle for what it does have.

above: Iron straps and hand painting mark this bed as original Monterey. A colored-pencil drawing of Tom Mix to the right of the bed seems a fitting reminder of the Monterey-Hollywood cowboy connection. **far left:** A stash of souvenir hats makes for an amusing and colorful collection. **left:** Later Monterey furniture incorporated an orange stain and a California palette of olive—as exemplified by the painted chair—Spanish red, and straw. **right:** Red-clay dinnerware comes in handy for alfresco dining and for a splash of color.

Monterey: The Best Of A Bygone Era

The Mason Manufacturing Company led the way in producing rustic-style furnishings between 1929 and 1943. Made from solid Oregon alder wood, some pieces were treated with an asphaltlike material that seeped into the wood like lacquer, rendering a dark, old-wood look. Other companies, such as Imperial, Montecito, and Coronado, introduced their own collections, but they could not replicate the quality of Monterey's ironwork, hand painting, and variety. Early pieces are heavy with iron hinges, latches, and strappings. They were branded with a horseshoe design and occasionally the word "Monterey." Some furniture had a small "M" on exposed nailheads. By the late 1930s, the furnishings incorporated purely Western motifs and tooled leather.

Design: South Of The Border

A departure from earthy Southwest tones, Mexican colors are exuberant—yellow, orange, blue, magenta, red, and hot pink. The colors fairly explode. Kitsch tourist pieces tend to be quirky and loud. Deep azure is reputed to ward off evil spirits. Mexican design celebrates the cycle of life. Motifs from nature include flowers, birds, and butterflies. In particular, monarch butterflies are highly regarded, for it is believed that every autumn they bear the spirits of departed relatives. During this season, Mexicans celebrate the holiday Los Dias de los Muertos, or "The Days of the Dead."

Chapter 4

Almost anything can be seen as "art" if *it's displayed* as such. A pair of farmer's overalls, starched and standing in a corner, becomes "sculpture." A WEATHERED SIGN assumes *new status* when proudly hung on a wall. Once-common glassware of the 1950s assumes the SOPHISTICATED presence of a *colorful painting* when displayed on glass shelves that become a room's FOCAL POINT. Use these

Collections
As Art

simple tips to give your *favorite things* star treatment:
• LIGHT OBJECTS to show off their artful details. Shine a spotlight on *wall-hung* objects. Add a strip light to set shelves aglow. Use a lighted pedestal *to display* pottery.
• GIVE TREASURES their own places to shine. See niches and shelves as frames; view hallways *as galleries*. Allow space between groupings so the eye can savor each special piece.

bottle cap sculpture

psychiatric-patient paintings

painted wood carvings

stone carvings

painted walking sticks

beaded suits

This St. Louis home exudes a *visual vitality*, tart and fresh, that HAS LITTLE TO DO with furniture or fabrics. It's *art that defines* the interior design of this house, but not just any art. The house is decorated ROOM TO ROOM, floor to ceiling with a *fine collection* of folk art, also known as "outsider art"—and the SPECIAL PASSION shared by John and Teenuh Foster. As a *trained painter* and practicing graphic designer, John appreciates THE FREEDOM OF

expression in works by *unschooled artists* often not formally recognized WITHIN THE MAINSTREAM gallery community. The *field isn't limited* to paintings, sculpture, or pottery. The Fosters also HAVE BIRDHOUSES that sprout antlers to look like fantasy *forest creatures*; SUITS OF CLOTHES that are truly buttoned up, with every thread of fabric *hidden beneath* an armor of sewn-on buttons; and OTHER TREASURES of wild imagining.

WHERE OUTSIDE IS IN

118

The antlered birdhouse is by Elwood Graham James (1890-1960), a West Virginia mute whose works have been exhibited in Europe. The sandstone carving, right, is by Gail Casilly and the painting by Chicago artist Michael Noland.

far left: Three crosses and carved baseball figures by Joe Hrovat adorn the bedroom dresser. **left:** Carvings by two Tennessee Appalachian farm families (the Webbs and Gibsons) stand beside a bottle cap windmill by Grace and Clarence Woolsey.

In some homes, the furniture is the focus, and the accessories are just that—colorful add-ons. The opposite is true in the Fosters' home, where the furniture takes second place to the folk art, which is the main event. By now, John and Teenuh's children—Hannah, 16, and Luke, 12—are used to their parents' unorthodox art. "They accept it, though they don't always understand it," Teenuh says. They're even less understanding about John's approach—a collecting method that makes outsider art a double entendre. Often, John ventures off the beaten path, on the prowl for a unique addition to his collection—and he takes the whole family with him.

"We've gone down many dirt roads with the kids on our summer vacations," he recounts, "and spotted yard art, whirligigs, or other unusual objects that require turning around to investigate. Sometimes the children see me crane my neck to look at something, and they'll say 'No way!' before I get the chance to stop. We have gone into neighborhoods that we were not too sure of in order for me to sit down and talk with an artist."

This hasn't always been the approach. While working on his master's degree in fine arts in drawing and painting, John traded art with his peers. In 1993, he saw his first true piece of folk art, and he was hooked.

"I loved the primitive, naive look. It feels so fresh and honest, particularly the art of the insane (an important category of outsider art). They had no knowledge of the gallery circuit and were doing this beautiful work because it was their means of expression. I just thought, that's the way to go. It is the real deal when you can make art for those reasons."

The Foster home is chock-full of self-taught art, from paintings by psychiatric patients and other naive canvases to bottle cap art, whirligigs, handmade game boards, as well as wheels, crosses, and mosaics.

"We look for work that's honest, extraordinary, and as far from contrived as possible," John says.

THIS IS THE CORNER TREE TO
HELL'S 20 ACRES AND IS KNOWN
BY THE HOODLUM AND THE THIEV-
ES ALL OVER THE USA THIS PLACE HAS
BEEN ROBBED OVER 50 TIMES IN THE
LAST 5 YEARS THE LAST TIME THEY MADE
A BIG HAUL WAS FEB 5TH 1961 THEY USE
WRECKING BARS SLEDGE HAMMERS HA-
MER & CHISEL THE BRAVE THING THEY STOLE
THE SHERIFFS NAME & THE SIGN THAT SAID TH-
AT THEY WERE NOT WORTH THE POWDER THAT

IT WOULD TAKE TO BLOW THEM TO
HELL I HAVE NEIGHBOURS AND FRIE-
DS WHO HAVE LOST OVER 50 HEAD OF
CATTLE STOLEN THERE HAS BEEN AS MU-
CH AS $1,000 REWARD FOR THE ARRE-
ST AND CONVICTION OF THESE CATTLE
ONE MAN OFFERED A REWARD OF $1,000 DOLL-
ARS NEVER HAVE HEARD OF JUST ONE HOOF
OR COWS FOOT EVER BEING RETURNED TO IT-
S OWNER I MY SELF HAVE LOST OVER 100 HEAD
OF CHICKENS AND DUCKS TRIED TO STEAL 2
POUND CALVES WHO WOULD NOT PAY ME

All Honor to the Ibn

A leather chair and ottoman add comfort but slip quietly into the background to allow one-of-a-kind folk art pieces to take center stage. A shards-mosaic coffee table and artfully crafted twig chair anchor the mix of handmade treasures.

THE ART OF THE
LONG M

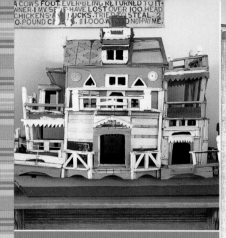

above: A colorful wooden boat by Louisiana self-taught artist J. P. Scott floats on a fireside table. right: The dining room's chandelier by John Baltrushunas of St. Louis includes old telescope lenses. Classic Craftsman-style furniture pieces set a mellow backdrop for the artwork the Fosters love. below right: A simple metal bed and soft taupe walls create serenity in the bedroom where wall art features an Amish game board. below: Standing guard in a hallway, the man's button suit was made in the 1940s by a woman from Council Bluffs, Iowa.

How You Play The Game

A 20th-century handmade gaming wheel by an anonymous maker points to one of John's most important collecting tips: Buy from a reputable dealer. John purchased this piece from Tim Chambers, an authority on early games. Chambers is the author of the new book *The Art of the Game Board*. John offers this second most important tip: Research the folk art genres in which you're interested. Check out websites, join a folk art organization, interview artists, and talk to dealers, in addition to reading books and magazine articles.

Making The Most Of Bottle Caps

This rabbitlike (or robotlike?) figure was among 100 pieces of bottle cap art by Grace and Clarence Woolsey. It was discovered in a barn after their deaths. The piece illustrates a guiding principle that John practices in his collecting: Search for the weird. "Within a specific folk art genre like bottle cap art or birdhouses, I like to look for the very weirdest examples that genre has to offer—the piece that really pushes the envelope," he says. He also advises collectors to buy for love, not money. "We never think about resale when we buy, even when it's quite an expensive piece," says John. "You should love it, or not buy it." Given several pieces to choose from by a single artist, always try to buy the best that your budget will allow.

Folk art and AMERICANA LIVE LARGE in Allan Katz's Connecticut farmhouse. This *nationally known* collector and dealer gives each piece the SPACE IT DESERVES to be fully appreciated, just as a *gallery owner* carefully POSITIONS PAINTINGS or sculptures. Allan makes a point of saying that *he learned early on* in his career to DISTINGUISH BETWEEN art and decoration. Three decades ago, *when Allan* was running a start-up electronics

 + 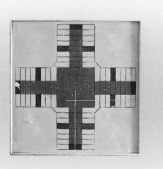 +  =

business, he fell for ADVERTISING MATERIALS and commercial tins. Given his *busy schedule,* acquiring this type of art was convenient because he COULD EVALUATE and *select pieces* mostly through the mail. Now he is a full-time dealer in the very materials he loves TO COLLECT. Allan's farmhouse—with *its white walls*, polished plank floors, and NATURAL LIGHT streaming in through 12-over-12 windows—is ideal for exhibiting his *distinctive art.*

PRISTINE FARMHOUSE

top: Objects are selectively positioned, as in this rare 19th-century weather vane above 1800s Acoma pottery. **above:** Massed collectibles, such as 19th-century commercial tins, sit evenly on shelves. **below:** A single 1820 redware jar pairs with a circa-1820 painted chest.

Allan Katz, one of America's leading collectors of folk art and Americana, refers to his collecting aesthetic as "lean, mean, and minimal." He sparely furnishes his farmhouse with objects he reveres as art. And in doing so, he imbues the structure with a surprisingly contemporary openness.

Allan prefers to group objects that "have some kind of harmonious relationship." His living room is awash in rare and colorful commercial art from the late 19th century. The eye skips from a dominant oil-on-canvas advertising sign for men's night robes to a massive plaster bust of a man sporting a top hat that promotes "Big Bill's Used Furniture."

It's not unusual for Allan to willingly share insights and anecdotes about almost every object in his house. A fetching cigar-store figure in a charming and rare cross-legged stance still has its original paint. "It's an accident that she was not ever repainted along the way," observes the dealer.

The one-of-a-kind weather vane—given a place of honor in the living room—is one of the collector's finest pieces. Dating from 1870, the figure above the vane's directional represents a Nipmuc tribal chief who is drawing back to shoot an arrow.

"You see the tension in his bow," says Allan, who, as a collector, aims for only the best. "For me it ranks at the top of the masterpiece pyramid."

Now a dealer of rare

This dealer *learned* early there's a difference between *art* and decoration.

Americana, Allan began collecting more than 30 years ago. Under the tutelage of Fred and Kathryn Giampietro, noted specialists in the field, he found a focus for his collecting.

"They showed me the difference between decoration and art," he remembers. "My eye took to it immediately."

A collector buys the object, not the story

The horizontal area above the mantel is ideal for a circa-1880s trade sign for a Maine excursion boat. A Pennsylvania cupboard shows off firkins and crocks used to promote Heinz Company condiments produced between 1883 and 1906.

left: Airbrushed Czech-German pottery has a sculptural effect when displayed on open shelving. right: A monumental circa-1915 photo relief bust, which the owner terms "early Pop art," contrasts with the simple lines of this 1880s deacon's bench.

behind it, asserts Allan. Nonetheless, the dealer's passion for collecting prompts him to discover all he can about his beloved objects. For example, by contacting a historical society in Virginia, he discovered that the cast-zinc lion presiding over his garden once sat atop the largest hardware store in the South. A City of New York document from 1899 helped him establish that a trade figure of a carved dog's head, another of his prized possessions, served

as the logo for a Brooklyn paint store.

Although an aesthetic object should be appreciated in and of itself, folk pieces and commercial art do offer a rich pictorial clue into American culture and history. Antique American folk art, which harkens back to the time of the early republic and even before, can be viewed as hands-on documentation of the American spirit. Mostly unknown artisans and craftspeople created objects at once utilitarian and attractive—whether

weather vanes, furniture, or pottery. Their intended audience, usually families and neighbors, was limited, yet meaningful. How shocked these craftspeople would be at the staggering prices now paid for some pieces.

Antique commercial art—a far cry from Madison Avenue and mass-media promotional glitz—also offers an intriguing window to lifestyles of the past. Signage, for instance, tells of products and

services used by our ancestors.

Ultimately, however, Allan's collecting is about art and individual taste. All collectors march to different drummers, he says. He recalls visiting an antiques show years ago at which an Englishman bought a medieval suit of armor.

"Can't you just feel the spirit of the warrior who took this into battle with him?" the man exclaimed to Allan.

"No," Allan replied, pointing to a fabulous weather vane across the aisle. "Now that makes my knees weak."

"Lean, mean, and minimal"—Allan's *secret* to *commercial* and folk art display.

Spare presentation continues in this bedroom, where a circa-1875 optician's trade sign of tin and glass graces an antique bed. A chest carved and painted in the cubist style anchors the foot, introducing an element of art dating before World War II.

groupings, clockwise from above left: The beauty of commercial art is in the details, whether in the shape of objects, images, or expression of message. Lithographs were made from this 1877 painting to promote train service from Chicago to destinations along Lake Michigan. A range of pieces adds diversity to this collection, from a late-1800s banjo chair and tambourine stool to condiment jars and a cigar-store princess. Individual style finds expression in a desk carved by a Norwegian American and a beehive in the likeness of a Civil War soldier.

Weather Vanes: Start In The Right Direction

These utilitarian pieces, made of metal or wood, are among the most popular Americana. Most before the Civil War were fashioned by hand. Motifs include farm animals, such as horses, cows, pigs, and roosters, as well as Indians. Antique weather vanes will not be in pristine condition, as they have endured exposure to outdoor elements. For example, copper ones have a green patina, and those made of iron develop a dark rust color. Wood weather vanes usually have cracks and edges that are worn and rounded. One side may show more wear and tear. Reproductions are common, so read and learn from knowledgeable dealers.

Artful Packaging Sends A Message

Collectible commercial art comes in various forms, shapes, and sizes. Tins are fun to collect, and the colors look great when a trove are lined on antique cupboards or distressed shelving. Such a display lends character to a kitchen or family room. Anyone wanting to know more about tins will find a variety of information and examples in *Antique Tins: Identification & Values* (1999). For those with a broad interest in commercial collectibles, The American Advertising Museum (www.admuseum.org) in Portland, Oregon, is a good starting point. It houses a comprehensive collection of artifacts.

Gaynell and Elias Hendricks consider AFRICAN ART their birthright. More than an *aesthetic delight* (though it surely is), AFRICAN ART IS a touchstone to their history—one they want to pass on to THEIR TWIN CHILDREN. "I want to surround *my children* with positive images of who they were," says Elias. He serves on THE CITY COUNCIL in Birmingham, Alabama, where *the family lives* in a downtown OFFICE BUILDING it purchased and converted *into*

apartments. In the Hendrickses' own apartment, the architecture is COOLLY MINIMALISTIC—a sophisticated approach designed to give the *intricate sculptural* shapes and VIVID, WARM COLORS of their collectibles every chance to shine. In what seems an unlikely *but successful* union, the AFRICAN ART pairs with Victorian furniture. *Curves and carving* connect ancient heritage, 19th-century flourishes, and NEW SOUTH SOPHISTICATION.

COMING FULL CIRCLE

A Nigerian earth mother ceramic sculpture by the Victorian chaise illustrates African art's communal, circular theme. Carved from a single piece of wood, the tree of life table displays Shoshona stonework from Zimbabwe.

It's no coincidence that most African sculptures and carvings are fashioned in the round. In the Hendrickses' collection, a queen's chair carved from a single piece of wood features a semicircle of standing figures with embracing arms as its back; a stone

From *great* suffering *comes* great art.

Shoshona earth mother sculpture is encircled with her children; the hand-carved tables and beaded stools are all round.

"In African cultures, everyone's life is part of the group," Elias explains.

African art reflects that philosophy, as do the Hendrickses' room arrangements. All their conversation groupings are circular—a reminder of the African emphasis on a close-knit community. A circular theme is even the collection's raison d'etre: Through their art, the Hendrickses travel full circle to reunite with the African culture from which they were cut off for so long.

That points to the most important reason for starting any collection— to gather objects that have personal meaning for you.

Elias' fascination with African art began in the 1960s, when he went to Africa with the Peace Corps. He quickly learned there's more to African art than those pieces created and marketed to the West during colonization. The Hendrickses' collection looks beyond the early 1900s to embrace art created both before and after imperialism reached its zenith. For instance, Gaynell's African doll collection in the living room is contemporary.

Like most zealous collectors, the Hendrickses started out collecting only objects imbued with special meaning, then meandered down other related avenues to expand their collections. Form creates continuity. "I like curves," explains Elias, pointing to the round-back Victorian seating that accompanies the African art. In addition, the

above left: Gaynell, who runs a chain of day care centers, expresses her love for children in a collection of dolls on a living room bench. **above:** An African queen's chair shares a corner with a Haitian painting and masks.

A Sierra Leone bust of Mammywata, a river goddess often shown draped with snakes, enlivens a Victorian end table. Ancestor statues from Cameroon climb the contemporary stairs, connecting the main floor and the upstairs.

Each piece in the *collection* is one more missing *link* to a lost ethnic heritage.

Architect David Gillespie designed a triangle of niches for displaying the Hendrickses' collection of small-scale Shoshona stonework, including busts, figures, and various vessels from Zimbabwe. Natural wood shows off dark sculpture.

couple's sophisticated design approach—using a uniform background of creamy walls and oak floors as a stage—spotlights the collection while unifying the home.

In the library, African pieces are presented with a collection of twig furniture crafted by a local artisan. Similar to the African wood furnishings carved from a single piece of wood, the twig furniture is made from long strands rather than smaller sections. Its handcraftsmanship increases the kindred spirit. This juxtaposition teaches an effective design lesson: Though objects may be disparate in origin, they may exhibit similarities in technique or construction.

After Gaynell and Elias launched their love affair with African art, they discovered that near look-alikes, not African, began to catch their eyes. Indonesian masks now join their art collection as an equally legitimate folk art form, even though devoid of African masks' personal legacy. Colorfully painted and collaged folk art sticks in the Hendrickses' collection aren't African either, but are the work of an African-American artist. In fact, Gaynell and Elias appreciate his work so much that it constitutes a mini collection within their larger one.

Contemporary busts of men and women join the art collection "because they remind me of a family member or even myself," says Elias. He says that he bought the bust on the table (shown right) because it resembled his uncle.

Curators assist in assembling certain pieces for the Hendrickses, but they ultimately rely on this well-worn scrap of logic: Buy what you like. No amount of rarity or technical mastery can compensate for a tug at the heartstrings.

The art spills onto walls, tabletops, and hallways, bringing style even to out-of-the-way places. African sculptures take to the stairs and landings. In a back stairwell, architectural niches house smaller art objects, inviting the eye to linger. In every room, this family's collection links it with ethnic history, making a bold statement in the present.

above: Beaded stools and a beaded chair from Nigeria and Cameroon join a collection of folk art sticks by Chris Clark and ornamental iron by metal artist Mustafa Abdulla. below: The throne chair is carved from one piece of wood.

137

above: Rustic and handmade, the library's twig furniture complements artwork that includes a Sierra Leone head, two altar pieces, a face jug by a local artist, a plate, a carved seated man, two ceremonial masks, and another new face jug. **far left:** Dolls on the top shelf were commissioned by an Ashanti king when his daughter died. They represent ideal beauty. **left:** These wall masks are Indonesian. **right:** Elias bought the seated carving because it reminds him of his grandfather. The mask next to it represents a king; the other is a Chokwe mask.

In The Art, We See Ourselves

Elias and Gaynell have gathered museum-quality African art into their Birmingham, Alabama, home. Their emphasis on quality pieces, however, hasn't hindered their foremost objective as collectors: They buy what moves them, and what moves them these days is anything, regardless of vintage or country of origin, that helps to flesh out their own identities as African-Americans and reinforce a positive self-image for their twin boy and girl. "I especially want to provide a positive image for my daughter," says Elias. "I buy anything I can find with strong female imagery." The contemporary bust of a woman sculpted in marble, shown here, is an example of African beauty. Elsewhere in the home, the family displays female deities and folk figures plucked from ancient African mythology, which is rich in female power wielders.

Masking The Differences

This mask is one of a collection of Indonesian face masks in the Hendrickses' art collection. At first, the presence of these non-African objects may seem incongruous, but that doesn't concern the Hendrickses, who see a stylistic and functional link between the two. After all, both African and Indonesian masks are in the genre of functional ceremonial art artifacts; both are handmade folk art; and both have an abstract expressiveness that appeals like modern art. Displayed together on a wall, the Indonesian masks make a collective statement and retain their integrity without being confused with the African masks that dominate the couple's collection.

A setting for *one-of-a-kind*, often offbeat arrangements of country collections doesn't GET MUCH BETTER than this. Mary Beth and Dan Sledge's *turn-of-the-century* farmhouse near Fredericksburg in the HEART OF THE Texas *Hill Country* has all the right ambience, starting with its tin siding and SCALLOPED TIN ROOF—an earful, come the spring rains. It's not just *charming features*, such as the PING OF RAIN on a tin roof, the home's 1908 vintage,

or even the region's dazzling *bluebonnets*, that make the home so ideal for its contents; it's the PERSONAL TOUCH of the owners. *The Sledges restored* the DILAPIDATED BUILDING by themselves. Every inch of floor, wall, and ceiling reflects a *labor of love*, and every room shows off a collection LOVINGLY GATHERED. In this context, *old silver*, aged sheet music, vintage Easter baskets, and other objects are UNIQUELY PRESENTED as art.

A TEXAS PATINA

Anything becomes art when treated as such. A silver tray and coffeepot are showcased by a vintage frame. Black-and-white family photos clipped to an antique chain transform the dining room's new chandelier into art.

top: Rusty keys dangle beneath creamy lace on a breakfast-room column. **above:** A $99 buffet from a Blanco, Texas, auction hosts pink Depression glass and silver. **below:** Animal McCoy pottery, postcards, and a Victorian camisole mix it up in the back entry.

"I like anything odd," says Mary Beth, who admits to agility in what she calls "the reach"—seeing decorative possibilities in the least likely places. Consider her collection of old tarnished teapots and coffeepots, for instance.

"Don't give me that shiny stuff!" she insists.

Standard thinking would have the vessels displayed on a shelf or tabletop, filing along in order according to size and shape. Standard thinking wouldn't embrace tarnished silver plate as a collectible in the first place. In Mary Beth's unique way of seeing, the pots—tarnish and all—become art when dangled in a cluster from hardware store link chains aged with a commercial soak.

The display calls to mind a kitchen rope of garlic or chiles with its casually strewn form. In this case, however, an unexpected elegance and beauty turn the dangling teapots into appropriate decorative fare for a formal dining room.

Mary Beth thickens the plot by suspending yet another dark-patina coffeepot on the adjacent dining room wall, this time in front of a hanging silver tray. Although floating from chains, both tray and teapot are "framed" by a beautiful antique picture frame—which also hangs from a chain. The wall itself serves as a mat.

The idea is clear: Almost anything can be art if treated as such. A foolproof approach is to display objects on the wall, as you would a painting. Tabletop collectibles, such as vintage silver baby cups (another of Mary Beth's collections—complete with dark spots), become art when chained, wired, or roped to the wall. To change the look, pretty grosgrain ribbon tied at the top into bows for English-style flair or raffia for a textural display may be used. In the bedroom, even a pair of children's chairs takes to the wall. These displays intrigue with surprise—three-dimensional objects in an arena that's usually flat-on-flat. In a wall composition of assorted silver platters, a little 3-D goes a long way: A butter dish in the dining room display works as a visual bump. It forces the

A creamy palette pulls together a mix of collectibles. Framed platters gain dimension and quirky interest with old keys as accents. One of a pair of columns made by Dan for their daughter's wedding holds a jumble of old white pots.

eye to brake—and appreciate.

Her idiosyncratic decorating proves that frames aren't just for paintings or photographs. Household serving pieces, however mundane, instantly gain status inside a frame: The framed trio of china platters in the breakfast room commands the same respect as an artist's canvas. In the living room, even a rusty old pressure gauge undergoes an artful metamorphosis, floating in front of an ornate picture frame. Mary Beth's loose interpretation of "framed" increases the visual interest: It's a treat to discover the framed object isn't lying flat on its back, pinned like a bug to the wall, but is flying in air.

It's possible to understand Mary Beth's eye for the unusual: Blame it on Mother.

"She's always been an inspiration to me in the decorating realm. When I was a small child, she was always moving things around or changing the appearance of items—cutting a kitchen table's legs down to turn it into a great sofa table, and turning an old radio cabinet into a side table. She had great style and was ahead of her time. She's where my love for the unusual and the 'reach' in decorating stems."

She's also the source of Mary Beth's collecting. Her mother gently nudged her at an early age into a lifetime habit. "She was an avid 'junk collector,' as my father would put it. She was always junking at garage sales and auctions." That example planted the collecting seed, and a gift at the age of 11 brought it to fruition. "I received an antique trunk full of vintage dishes and linens, silver flatware, and other incredible little trinkets. That really inspired me, and I began collecting old, wonderful things," says Mary Beth.

While she finds more collectibles all the time, she seldom lets go of any. The etched-glass creamer and sugar dish she received as an 11-year-old retain a special place on a kitchen shelf. For Mary Beth, they still work magic.

"I'm a *freak* about old Easter baskets—the *nostalgia*, I guess."

Old Easter baskets artfully blanket shelf space above freestanding bedroom closets. Hung as art, children's chairs, topped with their own Easter baskets and anchored by a lidded basket on the floor, add fresh dimension to the display.

groupings clockwise from above left:
Contrasting objects, such as keys trimming a lamp and old photos adorning a fixture, make a unique statement. Silver is an artful theme. Mary Beth procured the glass creamer and sugar dish as a child. Embroidery hoops and sheet music join creamware and Windsor chairs. A bowl and baby shoes create the unexpected, while yellowed book pages showcase chipped-paint metal. McCoy animals, beads, and photos make a whimsical display. A rusty bell and a pressure gauge hung as art lend charm to the living room.

With Imagination, Anything Goes

Mary Beth, a professional display artist for the last eight years, has no patience with people's self-imposed limitations. "This isn't the 1950s. We don't have to have matching shoes and bags! All we have to do is allow our imaginations to run a little wild with our displays." She freely mixes all manner of vessels, whatever their vintages, colors, and manufacturers. Creamy tones define her palette, but not obsessively. "Who cares if a water pitcher is white or cream? Use them all together." Her other tips for artful arrangements of potterylike water pitchers: Display in mass. Toss in a piece of vintage lace for softness. Fill with twigs and small, blooming tree branches instead of flowers.

Please Toss The Shiny Stuff!

Mary Beth's passion for silver plate is about appearances. She loves the mellow patina of the pieces—the gradual darkening, even black spotting, acquired over time. Collecting silver plate offers advantages over sterling: cost, availability, and easy maintenance. Silver plate costs a fraction of sterling, and it often can be found at yard sales. When appreciated for its aged look, it requires none of sterling's requisite polishing. As collectibles, silver tea and coffee services lend themselves to dramatic displays. Mary Beth advises filling a coffeepot with flowers or feathers, or piling beautiful old marbles into a silver sugar bowl.

Chapter 5

One of the *best contributions* collectibles make to any room is a sumptuous (and sometimes unexpected) INFUSION OF COLOR. Imagine a living room of white walls, beige carpet, and neutral upholstery. *Now consider* giving the room NEWFOUND SPIRIT with colorful Native American textiles, rugs, and pottery—or *kicking up* its energy level with hot orange or red glassware. DECIDE whether you want

COLOR CHOICES FOR
Collections

your collections to be a room's stars or its supporting cast.
● CHOOSE OBJECTS that set a palette and a mood. Try a yellow *McCoy cookie jar* on a rustic red bench below a Calder art print: DIFFERENT periods, same cheery feeling.
● LET COLLECTIONS echo a room's existing scheme and style. Blue and white transferware *plays to tradition*; bold Fiestaware enhances a BRIGHT SCHEME—country or modern.

pairs of figurines

heywood-wakefield furniture

rumrill pitchers

carnival chalkware

royal copley pottery

elephant planters

Rich Michels, the art director who *conceived and designed* this book, started buying 1950s FURNITURE just out of college. He preferred its "*more designed style*" over the boxy NEW FURNITURE available in the 1980s. Because retro *wasn't yet hot*, he had money to spare for 1930s to 1950s pottery. WHEN RICH MARRIED graphic designer Susan Uedelhofen and they *bought a house* in suburban DES MOINES, IOWA, his retro collections and her

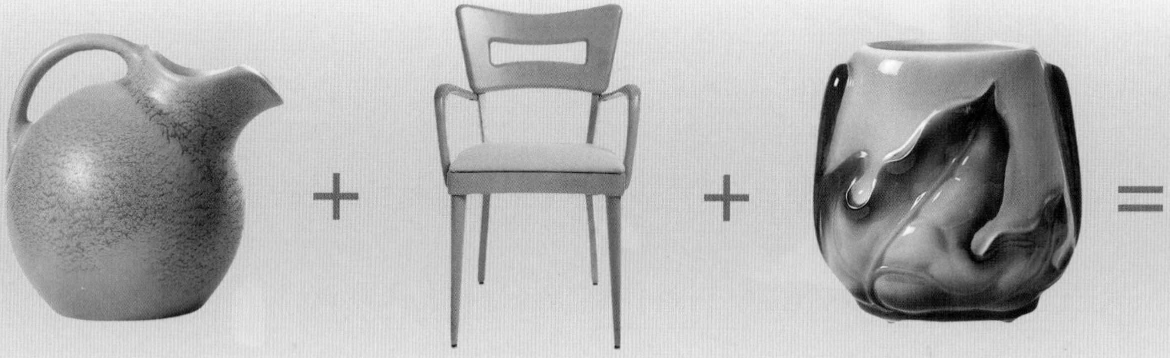

country primitives *weren't as compatible* as the couple. For harmony in the decorating, THEY DIVVIED up their house, *room by room*. Rich had more furniture, so retro won in the dining and living rooms, *his office*, and their master bedroom. To ENHANCE THE PRESENTATION, they matched room paint colors to the vintage *pottery glazes*: WALLS THE COLORS of water—turquoise, jade, and shades in between—*are as cool* as the collections themselves.

COLOR BY DESIGN

Rich bought the living room's Heywood-Wakefield bar and stools from his favorite local dealer. An organic theme dominates: It's in the leaf motif of the painting (artist unknown) and the Royal Copley pottery and lamps.

After a few secondhand 1950s purchases, Rich raised his design sights to blond Heywood-Wakefield furniture. "First it was a bedroom set, then dining room furniture, and then I was hooked," says Rich. His collection even includes a bar and barstools.

Getting each room's backgrounds just right to highlight the furniture was a priority. "The first order of business was to remove the wall-to-wall beige carpet and replace it with blond wood floors," recalls Rich.

The couple also stripped its home's dark woodwork to a honey blond to create a better blend with the retro furniture pieces.

Blond wood floors—or, where softness is needed, a pale area rug—blend smoothly with the furniture pieces.

Rich's collections dictate the design and color palette of each room in the home. In the living room, for example, one pair from his whimsical collection of vintage his-and-her figurines—this one, a pair of Spanish flamenco dancer lamps with bold color and plenty of attitude—inspired the entire room's spirited design.

"We chose red and green vintage upholstery to complement the lamps," says Rich.

Because vintage fabric is expensive, he recommends covering the sides, backs, and bottoms of cushions in complementary new fabrics and using the vintage fabric only on the tops of seat and back cushions.

The couple specifically selected the leaf pattern because it repeated the leaf theme of Rich's vintage Royal Copley pottery, which is displayed throughout the space. The leafy fabric added to the already breezy feel of the Heywood-Wakefield furniture and the bamboo loveseat and chair that Rich found at the Salvation Army. He painted the walls a warm green to pick up the tones of the pottery and plants.

Turquoise walls in the dining room exactly match the pottery displayed there. It's a "beautiful, cool backdrop for the warm wood tones," says Rich.

Gold, pattern-free upholstery on the chair

"With the *bamboo*, dancers, and the colors, the room feels like a *Polynesian* cabana."

Heywood-Wakefield tables are softened by a sea-grass area rug that underscores the room's cabana style. Rich stripped the windows to a lighter finish to better match the blond furniture, then left them undressed to simplify the space.

A rare Heywood-Wakefield corner cupboard joins a pedestal table and cutout chairs—all in wheat, the most yellow of the line's three finishes—in the dining room. The starburst fixture and mirror are both from the 1950s.

seats is a close match to the furniture's wood, keeping the emphasis on the sleek shapes of the sculptural chairs.

Because the decorating is simplified—essentially, the rooms offer a walk-in color study of the relationship between blue and blond—those collectibles that are more detailed carry more impact. A couple from Rich's vintage male-female figurines collection languidly observes table talk from atop a rare Heywood-Wakefield corner cupboard.

"That turquoise couple is one of my favorite pairs," says Rich. "I look for 'people' that look like they would fit in with the pairs I already have—like a Hollywood dinner party with guests who, though different, would have fun together."

Rich's upstairs office and paint studio showcases his collection of round pitchers, globes, and bowling balls.

"I've always been drawn to round objects," he explains. "The bowling balls started as a joke, but I loved the marble pattern. It's like marbles for grown-ups."

He considered painting the walls cobalt blue to pick up one of the vivid colors of the bowling balls and pitchers, but instead left them white as the cleanest background for his own colorful paintings. The white walls not only leave more latitude for color mixes among collectibles, but they allow each color to be fully appreciated. Carnival chalkware and Nemadji souvenir pottery collections, both brightly colored, sprawl across the room's shelves without looking busy.

Pale jade paint is the perfect foil for the bedroom's mix of stellar Heywood-Wakefield furniture and vintage pottery. The vanity—low, sleek, elegant, and with a grandly scaled mirror—is Rich's favorite furniture piece. Here, the couple's collections declare a truce: Susan's Frankoma pottery, a retro collection she started amassing after meeting Rich, looks at home on the headboard of his blond retro bed. Her pottery's soft green glaze even matches Rich's pair of vintage lamps.

top: The 1950s-vintage dishes in the hutch inspired the wall color. **above:** Susan is the country fan, but the primitive blue hutch was a mutual find. Collectible Chinese checkerboards add a touch of humor—and color.

155

Round objects—bowling balls, globes, pitchers—orbit a premier Heywood-Wakefield desk. Rich bought his first round pitcher for $2 to hold paintbrushes. Elephant planters above the window remind Rich of his childhood home.

Rich loves the *sleek* lines and curves of
the bedroom vanity and *kneehole* desk.

clockwise from top: As functional today as it was in the 1950s, the Heywood-Wakefield bedroom furniture is in the champagne finish—the palest available. Carnival chalkware is one of Rich's more recent collections. His metal state-shaped ashtray collection still lacks about 14 states. Rich's home office stores one of his favorite collections, round RumRill pitchers. Streaked Nemadji and other souvenir pottery, so known because the pieces were sold at tourist destinations, such as national parks, fills a shelving unit in Rich's office.

Not All Heywood-Wakefield Is Created Equal

The cutout armchair in Rich's dining room is one of Heywood-Wakefield's most collectible pieces. Such chairs were manufactured only from 1950 to 1955. Rich's pedestal dining table is newer, produced from 1956 to 1966. To collectors, the dining table and chairs are staples; Rich's desk, bedroom dresser, and corner cupboard are more important finds. Less prestigious pieces are those from the Ashcraft group, which include Rich's living room pieces. Ashcraft, made from ash, developed after rattan shipments were halted by World War II. Originally producing only summer or outdoor furniture, the company continued its manufacture after the war for indoors, including bedroom and dining room groups.

RumRill Or Red Wing?

The round pitchers Rich loves for their unique glazes and bulbous shapes are RumRill, a pottery produced exclusively by Red Wing from 1932 to 1937. The pottery's name comes from George Rumrill, who wasn't himself a potter but a broker of pottery. He marketed two lines of art pottery before entering into an arrangement with Red Wing. In 1935, both George Rumrill and Red Wing applied for a trademark on the RumRill name. Legal tussles followed, and both Red Wing and Rumrill's RumRill Pottery Co. of Little Rock, Arkansas, subsequently claimed to be sole licensees for the pottery. Collectors who love the pitchers aren't fazed by the confusion.

As an *interior designer*, Sonja Willman has an academic understanding of COLOR RELATIONSHIPS and the impact one *design element* has upon another. She also has a gift: She can mix patterns the way a PAINTER SWIRLS together pigments, with *equally assured* results. This sixth sense is at work in the 1919 NORMAN-STYLE home she and *her husband*, Bob, share in St. Louis. Her traditional English design is *peppered with* collections

of painted tole trays, STAFFORDSHIRE ANIMALS and figurines, majolica pottery, and *scenic-painted* English transferware—EACH COLLECTIBLE with a pattern of its own. Textiles take the mix up *several notches* to a dimension that is MANY LAYERS THICK. Plaids, tickings, florals, and toiles *work in tandem* with Sonja's collections in a style that's never busy, thanks to CAREFULLY COORDINATED color, and never boring, thanks to *sheer abundance*.

English Manners

Color relationships rule the living room. The browns of the tole trays repeat in the ticking that covers the walls. The walnut finish on the window and piano are a match. Glazes on the Staffordshire figurines appear on the pouf.

For Sonja, collecting and designing are alike. The collecting that started in her teens with gifts from cherished family members stretches to broader lengths today. "It's funny how some things you've never collected all of a sudden have an appeal. It's a love-hate relationship. I'm afraid to go shopping for fear of finding one more thing I like."

Apart from its collections, her home's design has an evolving life all its own. Sonja freely adds or subtracts fabrics or alters the look with a slipcover as inspiration strikes. Her fascination with the opportunity textiles present for playing with pattern, color, and texture developed about the same time as her collecting. "I always loved mixing patterns, and after college started putting different fabrics together in different ways. I like to see layers on layers of textures and colors." Sonja uses color to organize her mixes of patterns and collections. The tangy orange accent glaze on a collection of Staffordshire figurines gathered on her antique

piano corresponds to a paler extraction of the color on a plaid fabric shirred on the ottoman. Inky background colors on a collection of tole trays displayed on the wall blend with the darker glazes on the Staffordshire. The cream-and-brown ticking that covers the walls picks up the colors of the trays' painted flowers. What may seem as random as gathering wildflowers

"I like a handmade, *tactile* quality. I don't *mind* cracks and chips."

follows a chain of logic: One color leads deliberately, if subtly, to another so that no object, fabric, or furniture piece stands alone.

Sonja has a knack for building color relationships with ease. Anyone who can't do this so readily can employ a simple strategy: The trick is to consider how many other design elements

top: Artwork reflects the intricately worked wallpaper. A bamboo cupboard holds transferware. **above:** Two tiers of windows shower light on the living room for a British Colonial look underscored by old bamboo furniture.

The dining room alcove's frame of bright yellow wallpaper makes the niche—and the majolica collection displayed within it—a focal point. An antique Chippendale-style chair is from Sonja's collection of English classics.

"I'm *attracted* to the look of something.
It's not important *where* it came from."

Sonja carried the dining room's yellow and blue into the kitchen. She painted the home's original corner cupboards in an eye-popping mix of blue and yellow, then crowned their flat tops with a simple carved pediment for more graceful style.

any single collection's palette relates to within a space. When at least two other nearby elements (furniture, fabric, woodwork, art, or accessories) bear one of the colors, it's safe to assume a successful melding.

In the dining room, where Sonja displays her brilliantly colored majolica collection, the decorating keeps pace with its own fizzy palette. A scenic patterned reproduction wallpaper in bright yellow contains all the colors in the majolica, and the hues have similar brightness (color value) as those on the majolica. Having one decorative element (usually a wallpaper, fabric, or rug) contain all the colors in a room's palette ensures cohesion. Sonja's paper is detailed with figures, so to prevent confusion—and to up the color ante—she left it off the alcove walls where the majolica hangs. Instead, she painted the alcove blue— a clear sky to host her constellation of pottery.

The master bedroom and guest room return to the softer corals of the living room. The bedrooms' collections are

soft, romantic, and quintessentially English. Victorian shell art, antique bamboo campaign furniture, floral pictures, and vintage linens compatibly combine. Walls in both bedrooms feature coral as the rooms' dominant color; even shells and lampshades relate to it.

Sonja's evolution as collector and designer is best witnessed in the kitchen, which veers north of England to settle on a more Scandinavian style. She painted tall corner cupboards icy blue, and lightened up the furniture to all white for a Gustavian Swedish country look.

"I like the Scandinavian look, so maybe that's why I went this direction," she reflects. As with her collecting, her designing isn't as methodical as it is inspired: "I just relate to the things I collect, or they stir some kind of feeling." In the kitchen, her pattern-on-pattern montage of fabrics remains consistent with other spaces—just what you would expect of so masterful a mixer.

top: The butler's pantry, serving as a potting shed, is filled with a collection of old planters. Tin advertising signs provide a visual link to the kitchen's tins. **above:** Beneath a window, a collection of old tins makes a strong design statement.

165

above left: Solid coral-painted walls provide a simple background for the pattern mix of vintage quilts. above: The guest bedroom's toile wallpaper is a romantic fit for Victorian shell art and a French bamboo dresser. right: The green plate racks complement the majolica collection. below right: An Italian lamp decorated with children and flowers is part of a collection. below: Staffordshire spiel holders for rolled kindling papers reveal bright orange in their recesses. left: The chair echoes the mint green woodwork; the vase and prints, the yellow floral wallpaper.

Trace Art For Grown-Ups

English transferware begins when the design is traced over carbon paper placed on a copper plate. The lines are engraved, then shaded, and printing begins. Transfer-printed tableware dates to the late 1700s. To remove stains on all transferware other than hand-painted or gold-trimmed pieces, submerge the piece in a strong solution of hydrogen peroxide; soak up to a week. Then place the piece facedown on an aluminum-lined cookie sheet and bake at 200 degrees Fahrenheit for 1 to 3 hours. Allow to cool in the oven to avoid crazing. Rinse in warm, soapy distilled water.

Decorating With Colorful Majolica

Majolica's distinctive colors and shiny glazes have attracted collectors since the pottery was first produced on the Spanish island of Majorca, for which it was named. In the mid-1400s, Spanish potters exported their wares to Italy. Italy produced its own version, which surpassed the Spanish wares in number and fame. Majolica's unique look is achieved by glazing clay with a tin oxide to produce a soft white background. Designs in other metallic oxides are painted onto the white and turn bright colors when baked. True majolica is tin oxide-glazed Italian pottery, but the term often applies to molded English pottery. English "majolica" is usually larger and more decorative.

To think of S. Scott Mayers as a BIG-TIME COLLECTOR is to *think too small*. His collections don't span diverse categories. ANY DISCUSSION of size and scale in regard to Scott's collecting *requires pondering* an entirely different dimension. For, like NESTING BOXES, his myriad collections are CONTAINED WITHIN a collection—of circa 1915–1919 bungalows. He owns *three of them*, plus an old garage, all of which he has TURNED INTO A HOME for

himself and *his collections*, as well as an office for his practice as a PSYCHE-THERAPIST (he prefers the Greek term for "soul"). MAYERS' VENICE, California, compound—its sleeping, living, dining, and *working quarters* all connected by purple-stained decking—IS COLLECTIBLES-compatible by design. In keeping with *the spirit of* the COLLECTIONS THEMSELVES, boldly colored backgrounds for brightly hued collections *are the order* of the day.

BIG, BOLD, & BRIGHT

His mother's green candy dish (in the center of the mantel) started it all. Now Scott has a flock of such dishes, which look surprisingly contemporary in this spare context—a modern effect enhanced by the 1995 monoprints by Patricia Lazalde.

top: Many of the modern red vases are Blenko. above: Art Deco and Art Nouveau clocks started out helping Scott tell time in his practice, then grew to a collection. below: Orange agate and slag glass include pieces from Viking and Fenton, though most are unmarked.

"It is a kind of madness in a way," the mental-health professional suggests jokingly of his collecting habit. As proof, he appears to enter denial. "I don't actually consider myself a collector," Scott insists, gazing about the living room-kitchen bungalow, which is brimming with collections of Art Deco and Art Nouveau clocks, orange and red glass, cookie jars parading across the ceiling, and oddball furnishings retrieved from the trash. Not to worry. He can explain. "You get one, and then you get other ones, and then you somehow have a lot of them." Intent to collect must be present before one is guilty of being a collector, he reasons.

Surely, to be a real collector, one must love those items that one collects. Scott doesn't. "I've never had a great deal of attachment to the objects themselves. They are more like decoration for me—it's more about their value in interior design than about any intrinsic value."

His philosophy explains the importance of presentation—especially

colorful backdrops—to his collections. They have the most impact when massed in a single place, whether blanketing a wall or marching across a mantel. Scott's do both.

Solid backgrounds work better than pattern to show a collection because they permit a clean silhouette; not even a faux finish throws interference on Scott's walls. The collective statement becomes louder when backgrounds are brilliantly colored to make the pieces pop. (White walls make good, but less theatrical, foils.) Or walls can sport the same color as the collectibles for a pleasing blend.

Every wall and ceiling in Scott's house works with—or against—his collections, to create harmony or contrast. For example, strong backdrop color and unexpected placement enhance his cookie jar collection. The pieces skim along a shelf above louvered doors, where the ceiling ordinarily would be. (In the remodeling, Scott raised all the bungalows' ceilings to follow the pitch of the rooflines. This created extra air to prevent his collections

"Pieces come and go *according* to my whims, but that doesn't mean I lack *passion* about them."

A Chinese emperor chair is part of Scott's collection of furnishings saved from the trash. Now refinished, the chair shares a room with collections as diverse as cookie jars and modern orange glass. Bold wall colors pull it all together.

Reverse-painted silhouettes, one of Scott's favorite collections, work in tandem with a bright red wall to provide all the decoration needed in his bath. His arrangement takes the shape of a large square, not unlike a single piece of art.

"These things fall under the *heading* of *fashion* more than collection."

from appearing cramped, as well as unusual perches for objects.)

Grape-colored walls and a green ceiling make a zesty foil for Scott's collection of vintage wooden cigarette and Japanese puzzle boxes. The collectibles, some of which are also music boxes, congregate in a bamboo curio cabinet alongside furnishings from Scott's "garbage" collection: a molded-wood retro chair he found broken on a Hollywood sidewalk, then rescued and repaired, and an old folding screen he retrieved from the trash.

"I am a bringer-together ('how's that for slaughtering the language?' Scott laughs) of dead people's things, and in that way, their spirit is given new life."

The repetition of browns and beiges on the once throwaway furnishings and the boxes blends the collections; exuberant paint colors make them sing.

Scott's gathering of animal-shaped candy dishes started with a single piece from his mother. Each one a different color, the dishes are displayed on a mantel that Scott made

welcoming with bright, multicolored paints. Scott displays his "very Maxfield Parrish-esque" reverse-painted silhouettes en masse on a Chinese-red wall for the boldest effect.

In the bedroom bungalow, the funky nutcracker collection pops out from chocolate brown walls washed with mauve. Yet the collection "was never intended," Scott says. "It started accidentally, with one nutcracker given to me as a gift." Now he plans to sell. "Out with the old, in

with the new," he says.

He suggests another reason for his acquisitive behavior: the love of the hunt. "It's the act of finding and collecting that I love, more than objects themselves," Scott says. "This habit is probably leftover from a primitive hunter-gatherer instinct. I've been going to garage sales and flea markets for as long as I can remember. To me, it is entertainment."

Spoken like a true collector.

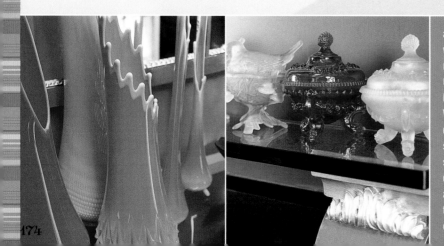

above: The cacophony of color created by the wooden nutcrackers on the nightstand is repeated in the room's artwork. **far left:** Orange agate and slag glass look like marble but were sold at five and dimes. **left:** Westmoreland Glass Company candy dishes date from the 1920s to 1950s. They assume a sculptural effect when displayed on a glass shelf. **right:** Some of the wooden boxes deliver a cigarette and a tune at the touch of a button. Because they share the same wood tones and are displayed together, the boxes create cohesiveness, not clutter.

Portrayed In Striking Silhouette

Reverse-painted silhouettes are a throwback to a more romantic era. Each painting on glass features dreamy characters—women in billowing skirts or men in seafaring costume—silhouetted against an idyllic landscape or seascape. The pictures' distinct look was created by painting a scene on the curved back side of the glass, so it shows through, yet is protected. Most of the works date to the early 1900s, with some as late as 1940. When Scott began collecting, he "was paying next to nothing." Now a single silhouette painting costs $70 or more. When collecting, look for similar framing treatments. All of Scott's silhouettes amazingly feature identical scrolled-metal frames, which he has left unchanged—part of the display's charm.

Hands Off The Cookie Jars

There's an entirely different reason to stay away from these cookie jars besides spoiling your dinner: fear of breaking these valuable collectibles. It all started when Andy Warhol sold off his collection for around $3 million. "That set the whole pace," says Scott. "What used to be a throwaway item now had some sort of cachet." Cookie jars are still easy to find, though their dollar days are long gone. Jars in mint condition can bring triple the price of the same imperfect piece. Take care to know a reproduction from a vintage piece. Look for signs of wear along the base, but be aware that even this can be faked. Visit reputable dealers to learn the old from the new.

A Cape Cod-style house *speaks of tradition*—boxy balance, ɢᴀʙʟᴇᴅ ᴅᴏʀᴍᴇʀꜱ, and pilasters framing the front door. Sara and David Gomez, however, *have checked* ᴘʀᴇᴅɪᴄᴛᴀʙɪʟɪᴛʏ at the threshold of their 1939 cottage in Portland, Oregon. Step inside and *spontaneity rules*. Moving from a *larger home* forced creative decision-making so the couple could fit in ɪᴛꜱ ᴄᴏʟʟᴇᴄᴛɪᴏɴꜱ; but *instead of* sweating it, the two dove in enthusiastically.

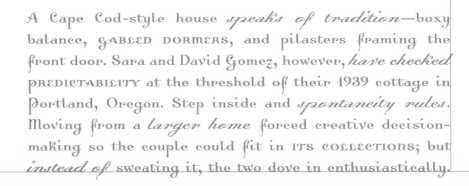

They took *their color cues* from the rainbow hues of their 1930s and 1940s pottery. Sara also ʀᴇʟɪᴇᴅ ᴏɴ ᴛʜᴇ sensibilities of her *graphic-designer* husband, though she ꜰᴏʟʟᴏᴡᴇᴅ ʜᴇʀ own instincts, as well. "There's nothing scientific, planned, or *predestined about* my collecting," she says. Relying on a ᴘᴀꜱꜱɪᴏɴ ꜰᴏʀ ᴛʜᴇɪʀ ᴄᴏʟʟᴇᴄᴛɪʙʟᴇꜱ and a *penchant for playfulness*, they have created an ɪᴍᴀɢɪɴᴀᴛɪᴠᴇ ꜱᴇᴛᴛɪɴɢ within an ordinary structure.

The Chic Of Shabby

The homeowners practice an open-door policy in their sunny kitchen. A deep chair invites visitors to plop down. Wall-mounted shelves show off curvy McCoy vases, even as a quilt-draped ladder lends a vertical, albeit amusing, touch.

Oregon weather can be overcast and rainy. When the clouds roll in, the Gomez family still gets a healthy dose of light and color, thanks to its fresh blend of pottery, distressed furnishings, fabrics, and other objects.

In moving from a large home to a smaller one, the Gomezes did not impose a lot of rules. Overly thought-out design never occurred to this energetic couple.

"We had no idea how our stuff would line up," says Sara. "We just got in here and went with it."

Yellow, green, blue, and airy white—colors resonating in their collections—form the basis of the dominantly pastel color scheme. For instance, blue-green walls contrast with yellow fabrics plus some blues and whites. In the kitchen, shades of yellow reign, with dashes of blue and green, and hints of red.

Although they are not longtime collectors, Sara and David have built a nice collection of American pottery, which they enjoy every day instead of closeting it away. A collection of paint-peeling cupboards and tables offers places for display throughout the house. The turquoise door of an armoire is thrown open to reveal a mix of McCoy pottery, stacked books, and silver candelabra. Wall-mounted shelves are loaded with yellow McCoy pieces and topped with a row of maple syrup cans in the kitchen, while old shelves in the dining room hold all manner of white matte pottery, including USA, McCoy, and Bauer. Flowers spring cheerfully from a row of pottery jardinieres on a rustic bench in the living room—no window treatments necessary.

Furniture is never typecast in this house. A pie safe sits in the master bedroom. An architectural remnant that hangs over the kitchen's French doors originally was planned for the master bedroom but ended up a misfit. Sara didn't rush into figuring out what to do.

"It stayed outside on the deck for weeks, until I finally brought it into the kitchen," she says.

Her lighthearted approach makes mingling pieces a pleasure, never an issue. Objects of the

Color, *mixing* of collections, and spontaneity offset Oregon's *overcast* weather.

Bright jardinieres in the window juxtapose with softly slipcovered furnishings and distressed woods. A dark wicker chair makes a contrasting statement in texture when set in front of a smooth pastel-painted folding screen.

This relaxed style instantly communicates comfort and creativity. An old oak French wine-tasting table makes the dining room distinctive, especially when grouped with a half-dozen chairs painted in sherbet hues.

heart embellish other surfaces with ease. On the mantel, oil paintings of flowers, pleasantly faded with age, square off against mercury glass balls and green McCoy pieces—a friendly competition of shape, size, and color.

Sara softens her style with loose slipcovers, a practical and pretty decorating solution for a young family.

"All our fabrics are washable," she says. "With two basset hounds and a 6-year-old, hardwood floors are a must. It's all about ease."

She taps her ingenuity when working with fabrics. Loving the festive flavor of tablecloths from the 1940s and 1950s, Sara stacks them in cupboards for display.

She also repurposes fabrics cleverly. She does not hesitate to eclectically combine color and pattern. For instance, Sara had taupe and yellow materials stitched together and trimmed with yellow cording for curtain panels in the master bedroom.

"It's like working a puzzle," she says. "You play with the pieces until they fit."

Another case in point is the shade she had made for a floor lamp. From her ever-ready stash of textiles, she chose an old-fashioned fabric with a creamy background and whispers of red in oversize flowers. Pastel blue-green fringe adds airy romance.

The master bedroom is a retreat of plump pillows, layered comfort and textures, and timeworn painted furniture. To introduce an accent color into the room's monochromatic palette, Sara topped a petticoat-full bed skirt and silver chenille duvet cover with an Amish star quilt trimmed in pale blue. This dark tone, echoed in the bed frame, visually anchors the pale, almost ethereal setting.

Sara's free expression is a fascinating counterpoint to her professional background in computer science. Yet a career change may be down the road. "I'd love to open a shop and carry artwork, antiques, fabrics, and vintage collectibles," she says. With the practice she's had incorporating treasures into her own house, that dream may well come true.

above: Painted furnishings with colors akin to their favorite pottery are part of Sara and David's collections. Seashell motifs lightly accent tabletops. **below:** An alternating parade of pottery and artwork follows the line of the staircase.

clockwise from top: Sara cleverly used vintage fabrics to make curtains and the shade for this floor lamp. A basket shelf was hauled up from the basement to add storage space and style to the master bath. Fabrics from the 1940s and 1950s often turn up at markets and antiques malls. Sara collects napkins if tablecloths are pricey. Old painted shelves display white matte pottery, including USA, McCoy, and Bauer. An Amish star quilt tops a silver chenille duvet cover, creating textural interest and accenting the monochromatic palette.

Looking For
The Real McCoy

McCoy mania has swept the country. If you're warming up to its happy hues, wise up to the fakes by remembering a few tips when you're on the prowl. Real pieces are typically white, maroon, cobalt, deep yellow, and aqua. If you fall for pink, light yellow, blue-speckled white, lime green, or light blue pottery, resist. Knockoffs may be white or aqua, so be prudent and closely examine pieces. Fakes may be off in size; ask the seller for exact measurements. Pottery made before 1938 does not bear marks. Though visible on pieces produced in later years, they vary. Read references and talk to trustworthy dealers.

Gently
Care For Oil Paintings

Treat oil paintings with kindness, giving as much thought to their protection as to aesthetic statement. Avoid hanging your art in direct sunlight, for it can fade pigments and increase the yellowing of old varnish. Extremes in temperature and humidity also can cause damage. For example, paintings may suffer near heating and air-conditioning vents or in a bathroom with a tub or shower. You need only dust every few months or so; a makeup brush will not scratch the surface. It's wise to consult a trained conservator for repairs, such as flaking, discoloration, tears, mold, or dirt.

Shopping

Interesting shops, shopping districts, and flea markets abound from coast to coast. Use this sampling as the starting point for your own great treasure hunt.

ALABAMA
Birmingham Antique Mall
2211 Magnolia Ave. S.
Birmingham, AL 35205
205/328-7761
Scottsboro Flea Market
Scottsboro, AL
Year-round
First Monday of the month and
the preceding weekend
800/259-5508

ARIZONA
Piney Hollow
427 N. Fourth Ave.
Tucson, AZ 85705
520/623-4450
Tres Encantos
La Plaza Shoppes
6538 E. Tanque Verde, Suite 110

Tucson, AZ 85715
520/885-4522
Neighborhoods & Districts
Tucson, AZ:
•Fourth Ave. district
•Plaza Palomino, Swan at Fort
Lowell
•St. Philips Plaza, River Rd. and
Campbell Ave.

CALIFORNIA
Interieur Perdu
340 Bryant St.
San Francisco, CA 94107
415/543-1616
Ohmega
2407 San Pablo Ave.
Berkeley, CA 94703
510/843-7368
Omega Too

204 San Pablo Ave.
Berkeley, CA 94702
510/843-3636
Pasadena Swallowtail
2217 Polk St.
San Francisco, CA 94109
415/567-1555
Rose Bowl Flea Market
Pasadena, CA
Year-round
Second Sunday of the month
323/560-7469
Treasure Island Flea Market
San Francisco, CA
Year-round
Sundays
415/255-1923
Trout Farm
1649 Market St.
San Francisco, CA 94103

415/626-1599
Zonal
568 Hayes St., off Laguna
San Francisco, CA 94115
415/255-9307
Districts & Neighborhoods
•Fourth St. area,
Berkeley, CA

Connecticut
Farmington Antiques Weekend
Farmington, CT
Second weekend in June
and Labor Day weekend
317/598-0012
www.farmington-antiques.com

District of Columbia
Gore Dean Antiques
1529 Wisconsin Ave. NW
Washington, DC 20007
202/625-1776
Districts & Neighborhoods
•Georgetown, particularly
Wisconsin Ave.

Florida
Renninger's Florida Twin Markets
Mt. Dora, FL
Year-round
Fridays, Saturdays, Sundays

Georgia
Lakewood Antiques Market
2000 Lakewood Ave. SE
Atlanta, GA 30315
404/622-4488
Scott Antique Mart
3850 Jonesboro Rd. SE
Atlanta, GA 30354
404/363-0909
Districts & Neighborhoods

Atlanta, GA:
•Buckhead area (specifically
Miami Cir., Bennett St.,
•N. Highland Ave. NE)
•Virginia-Highlands area
•West End area, Howell Mill Rd.
NW

Illinois
Antiques Market I
Market I
First N. Third St.
St. Charles, IL 60174
630/377-1868
Antiques Market II
301–303 W. Main St.
St. Charles, IL 60174
630/377-5818
Antiques Market III
413 W. Main St.
St. Charles, IL 60174
630/377-5599
Architectural Artifacts, Inc.
4325 N. Ravenswood
Chicago, IL 60613
773/348-0622
Daniel's Antiques
3711 N. Ashland Ave.
Chicago, IL 60613
773/868-9355
Dearborn House Antiques and Garden
116 State Ave.
St. Charles, IL 60174
630/762-1034
Decoro
2000 W. Carroll Ave., #503
Chicago, IL 60612
312/850-9260
Decoro
224 E. Ontario St.
Chicago, IL 60611
312/943-4847

Gabriel's Trumpet
229 Rice Lake Sq.
Wheaton, IL 60187
630/871-9500
Grayslake Antiques
Collectibles and Flea Market at
the Fairgrounds
Grayslake, IL
Year-round
Second Sunday of the month
847/223-2204
Griffins & Gargoyles, Ltd.
2140 W. Lawrence Ave.
Chicago, IL 60625
773/769-1255
Johnson's Statuary
316 Cedar St.
St. Charles, IL 60174
630/584-1571
Kane County Flea Market
Kane County Fairgrounds
St. Charles, IL
Year-round
First weekend of the month
630/377-2252
www.kanecountyfleamarket.com
**Mike Bell Antiques &
Reproductions**
111 N. State St.
Chicago, IL 60602
312/781-5713
Pagoda Red
1714 N. Damen
Chicago, IL 60647
773/235-1188
Pavilion Antiques
2055 N. Damen Ave.
Chicago, IL 60647
773/645-0924
Towns, Districts, & Neighborhoods
•Geneva, IL
•Sandwich, IL

 +  +  + 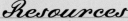 +

Resources

Indiana

Borkholder Dutch Village
71945 C.R. 101
Nappannee, IN 46550
219/773-2828
www.borkholder.com
Towns, Districts, & Neighborhoods
•Old Metamora, IN
•Shipshewana, IN

Iowa

Alverda's Antiques
211 Fifth St.
West Des Moines, IA 50265
515/255-0931
AOkay Antiques
124 Fifth St.
West Des Moines, IA 50265
515/255-2525; 800/968-4993
Banowetz Antique Mall
Hwy. 61 & Hwy. 64 Junction
Maquoketa, IA 52060
563/652-2359
www.banowetzantiques.com
Collector's Paradise Flea Market
20 miles south of I-80, Hwy. 21
First weekend in May, August,
October
641/634-2109
Christine's
309 E. 5th St.
Des Moines, IA 50309
515/243-3500
Elinor's Wood'N Wares
102 Fifth St.
West Des Moines, IA 50265
515/274-1234
**Historic Valley Junction Antiques
Jamboree**
Second Sunday of June, August,
and September
West Des Moines, IA

515/222-3642
Majestic Lion Antique Center
5048 Second Ave.
Des Moines, IA 50313
515/282-5466
www.majesticlion.com
Pappy's Antique Mall
103 First Ave. W.
Newton, IA 50208
641/792-7774
Sisters Garden
4895 Hwy. One SW
Kalona, IA 52247
319/683-2046
Vandeest Antiques at Calder Cottage
1216 Second Ave. SE
Cedar Rapids, IA 52403
319/286-8133
Towns, Districts, & Neighborhoods
•Amana, IA
•Clear Lake, IA
•Kalona, IA
•Walnut, IA

Kansas

Mission Road Antique Mall
4101 West 83rd St.
Prairie Village, KS 66208
913/341-7577

Kentucky

October Court Days
Mount Sterling, KY
Third Monday in October and
the preceding weekend
859/498-5343

Maine

Towns, Districts & Neighborhoods
•Wells, ME
•Kennebunkport, ME

Maryland

Mid-Atlantic Antiques Market
West Friendship, MD
Last Sunday in March and
October
410/228-8858
Towns, Districts, & Neighborhoods
Frederick, MD
Kensington, MD

Massachusetts

Abodeon
1731 Massachusetts Ave.
Cambridge, MA 02138
617/497-0137
**Brimfield Outdoor Antiques and
Collectibles Show**
Brimfield, MA
May and September. Check
website for dates.
www.brimfield.com
Fresh Eggs
58 Clarenden St.
Boston, MA 02116
617/247-8150
Todd's Farm Flea Market and Antiques
Rowley, MA
Sundays, April to Thanksgiving
978/948-3300
Towns, Districts, & Neighborhoods
•Sheffield, MA

Michigan

Allegan Antiques Market
Allegan, MI
Last Sunday of the month, April
through September
616/735-3333
Dunes Antique Center
12825 Red Arrow Highway
Sawyer, MI 49125
616/426-4043

 + 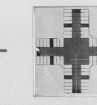 +  +  +

Harbert Antique Mall
13887 Red Arrow Hwy.
Harbert, MI 49115
616/469-0977
Springdale Furnishings
19 S. Elm
Three Oaks, MI 49128
616/756-9896
Van Daff's Interior Design and
Antiquities
2120 Wealthy SE
East Grand Rapids, MI 49506
616/456-0532
Districts & Neighborhoods
Harbor Country, Southwest
Michigan
www.harborcountry.org

Minnesota
Districts & Neighborhoods
Minneapolis/St. Paul, MN:
•Hennepin Ave.
•Lake St.
•Lyndale St.

Missouri
Fellenz Antiques
439 N. Euclid Ave.
St. Louis, MO 63108
314/367-0214
Geronimo's Cadillac
4735 McPherson Ave.
St. Louis, MO 63108
314/863-4233
Warson Woods Antique Mall
10091 Manchester Rd.
St. Louis, MO 63122
314/909-0123
West End Gallery
4732 McPherson Ave.
St. Louis, MO 63108
314/361-1059

Districts & Neighborhoods
Greenwood, MO:
•Grand Ave. area
Kansas City, MO:
•Country Club Plaza, Crestwood
•Shops, 55th St. between
Brookside and Oak, Crossroads
•District, River Market

Nebraska
Districts & Neighborhoods
Omaha, NE
•Old Market area

New Hampshire
Antiques Week in New Hampshire
Manchester, NH
Week after the first Saturday in
August
207/767-3967
Barn Antiques
44 Lafayette Rd.
Hampton Falls, NH 03844
603/926-9003

New Jersey
Atlantique City Holiday Megafair
Atlantic City, NJ
March and October
800/526-2724

New Mexico
Pegasus Antiques
Call for directions and
appointment.
Santa Fe, NM
505/982-3333
Santa Fe Antiques Show
Sweeney Convention Center
Santa Fe, NM
July and December
Call for dates: 505/753-2553

Trader Jack's Flea Market
U.S. Hwy. 84/285
6 miles north of Santa Fe, NM
Districts & Neighborhoods
Santa Fe, NM
Canyon Road

New York
Annex Antiques Fair and Flea Market
6th Ave. from 24th to 27th Sts.
New York, NY
212/243-5343
Rhinebeck Antiques Fair
Rhinebeck, NY
Memorial Day weekend, fourth
Saturday in July, and Columbus
Day weekend
845/876-1989
Soho Antiques Fair
Corner of Broadway and Grand
St., 2 blocks north of Canal St.
New York, NY
212/682-2000
Towns, Districts, & Neighborhoods:
•Hudson, NY
•Saugerties, NY

North Carolina
Great American Antiques Spectacular
Charlotte, NC
April, June, and November
First Saturday of the month and
the preceding Friday
704/596-4643 or 800/824-3770

Oklahoma
Deco to Disco
2921 E. 15th St.
Tulsa, OK 74120
918/749-3620
Tulsa Flea Market
State Fairgrounds

Resources

21st St. and Yale
Tulsa, OK 74112
Towns, Districts & Neighborhooods
•Jinx, OK

OREGON
Gilgamesh
2800 NE Sandy Blvd.
Portland, OR 97232
503/233-1890
Star Antiques
7030 SE Milwaukee
Portland, OR 97202
503/235-5990
Star Antiques
7027 SE Milwaukee
Portland, OR 97202
Star Antiques
6717 SE Milwaukee
Portland, OR 97202
503/235-9142

PENNSYLVANIA
Renninger's Antique Market
Adamstown, PA
Year-round
Sundays
717/336-2177
Renninger's Antiques, Collectibles, and Farmer's Market
Kutztown, PA
Last full weekend in April, June, and September
877/385-0104

SOUTH CAROLINA
Croghan's Jewel Box
308 King St.
Charleston, SC 29401
843/723-6589
Golden & Associates Antiques, Inc.
206 King St.

Charleston, SC 29401
843/723-8886
Michael Rainey Antiques
702 Craven Street
Beaufort, SC 29902
843/521-4532
Queen Charlotte Antiques, Ltd.
173 King St.
Charleston, SC 29401
Districts & Neighborhoods
Charleston, SC
•King Street

TENNESSEE
Heart of Country
Opryland Hotel
Nashville, TN
Mid-February, mid-October
Call for dates: 800/862-1090
Towns, Districts, and Neighborhoods:
•Franklin, TN

TEXAS
Canton Market
Canton, TX
Year-round
Thursday through Sunday before the first Monday of the month
903/567-6556
Cierra Furniture
2920 N. Henderson Ave.
Dallas, TX 75206
214/887-8772
David Lackey Antiques
2311 Westheimer Rd.
Houston, TX 77098
713/942-7171
Jewels & Junque
2715 Broadway St.
Galveston, TX 77550
409/762-3243
Kay O'Toole Antiques & Eccentricities

1921 Westheimer Rd.
Houston, TX 77098
713/523-1921
Kuhl-Linscomb Antiques
5120 Woodway Dr.
Houston, TX 77056
713/840-1500
La Hacienda Furnishings
14028 Memorial Dr.
Houston, TX 77079
281/589-6990
Love's Field Antique Mall
6500 Cedar St.
Dallas, TX 75235
214/375-6500
R. Harold Hollis Antiques
21309 Cy. Rd. 456
Normangee, TX 77871
936/396-1246
Round Top Antiques Shows
Round Top, TX
Call for dates: 979/249-4042
Districts & Neighborhoods
Houston, TX:
•19th St. area, between Studewood and Heights Blvd.
•Rice Village, off Kirby in W. University area

VIRGINIA
Futures Antiques
3824 Granby St.
Norfolk, VA 23504
757/624-2050
Lucketts Store
42350 Lucketts Rd.
Leesburg, VA 20176
703/779-0268
The Richmond Antiques Spectacular
The Showplace on Rte. 360 E
Richmond, VA
One weekend a month in

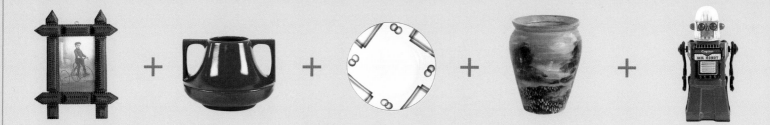

January, February, March, June, September, and November
804/462-6190
Twig House
132 Maple Ave. East
Vienna, VA 22180
703/255-4985
Town, Districts, & Neighborhoods
•Leesburg, VA
•Warrenton, VA

Washington
Current and Current/Details
629 Western Ave.
Seattle, WA 98104
206/622-2433
David Smith and Company
334 Boren Ave. N
Seattle, WA 98109
206/223-1598
A Garden of Distinction
5819 Sixth Ave. S.
Seattle, WA 98108
206/763-0517
www.agardenofdistinction.com
Veritables
2816 E. Madison St.
Seattle, WA 98122
206/726-8047
Districts & Neighborhoods
Seattle, WA
•Pike Place Market area

Canada
Districts & Neighborhoods
Montreal, Quebec:
Antique District
Victoria, British Columbia:
Antique Row
Fort St.
Vancouver, British Columbia:
Granville Island

Internet Search Tips for Antiques and Collectibles
•www.FleaMarketGuide.com
•Keywords: Use "antiques," "flea markets," or object names.
•Internet yellow pages: Use a search engine, such as dogpile.com, click on Yellow Pages, and search for antiques dealers by city.

House Credits
Pages 12-21, Cluster and Conquer
Regional Editor: Barbara Mundall; Photography: Jon Jensen
Pages 22-29, Quirky Americana
Regional Editor: Heather Wright Lobdell; Photography: Jeff McNamara
Pages 30-39, Indulging in Deco
Photography: William Hopkins
Pages 40-45, Cottage by the Sea
Regional Editor: Nancy Ingram; Photography: Hal Lott
Pages 48-55, An Evolving Eye
Regional Editor: Mary Anne Thomson; Photography: Alise O'Brien
Pages 56-65, All in the Blend
Regional Editor: Andrea Caughey; Photography: Edward Gohlich
Pages 66-71, A Texan's Roundup
Regional Editor: Joetta Moulden; Photography: Fran Brennan
Pages 72-79, Cool Kitsch Rules
Regional Editor: Diane Carroll; Photography: Jenifer Jordan
Pages 82-89, Southern Refined
Photography: Coleen Duffley

Pages 90-95, Minimal Artifacts
Regional Editors: Sally Mauer and Hilary Rose; Photography: Jon Miller, Hedrich-Blessing
Pages 96-101, A Magical Escape
Regional Editor: Carla Breer Howard; Photography: Jon Jensen
Pages 102-109, Focus on the Fifties
Regional Editor: Hilary Rose; Photography: Peter Walters
Pages 110-115, California Rustic
Regional Editor: Mary Anne Thomson; Photography: Philip Clayton-Thompson
Pages 118-123, Where Outside is In
Regional Editor: Mary Anne Thomson; Photography: Alise O'Brien
Pages 124-131, Pristine Farmhouse
Regional Editor: Trish Foley; Photography: Jeff McNamara
Pages 132-139, Coming Full Circle
Regional Editor: Debra Hastings; Photography: Sylvia Martin
Pages 140-147, A Texas Patina
Regional Editor: Nancy Ingram; Photography: Gordon Beall
Pages 150-159, Color by Design
Photography: William Hopkins
Pages 160-167, English Manners
Regional Editor: Mary Anne Thomson; Photography: Alise O'Brien
Pages 168-175, Big, Bold, & Bright
Regional Editor: Laura Hull; Photography: Mark Lohman
Pages 176-183, The Chic of Shabby
Regional Editor: Donna Pizzi; Photography: Philip Clayton-Thompson

 +  +  +  +

Index

 +  + 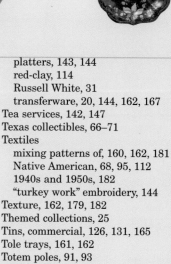 + 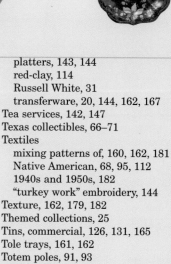 +

 +  +  +  +  +

Collector's Style~

chairs • 1940s vases • doll beds • vintage trunks • old postcards • carved hands • toy robots • missouri pine
globes • roseville pottery • red wing pottery • bluebonnet pottery • landscape paintings • texas biedermeier
ooks • state plates • swizzle sticks • japanese ikebana baskets • architectural fragments • looking glasses
sculptures • japanese antiques • italian seating • theatrical posters • automata • victorian books • magic sets
niture • wedgwood pottery • barbecue trays • mexican kitsch • red-clay dinnerware • monterey furnishing
wood carvings • stone carvings • painted walking sticks • beaded suits • redware pottery • wooden signs
e • face jugs • shoshona stonework • painted sticks • easter baskets • depression glass • tarnished silver
rnival chalkware • royal copley pottery • tole trays • staffordshire pottery • majolica • english transferware
s • nutcrackers • mccoy pottery • maple syrup cans • oil paintings • vintage textiles • antique cupboards
ctorian carpet balls • mocha ware • treenware • bandboxes • folk art frames • cocktail shakers • cobalt glass
t chairs • 1940s vases • doll beds • vintage trunks • old postcards • carved hands • toy robots • missouri pine
globes • roseville pottery • red wing pottery • bluebonnet pottery • landscape paintings • texas biedermeier
ooks • state plates • swizzle sticks • japanese ikebana baskets • architectural fragments • looking glasses
sculptures • japanese antiques • italian seating • theatrical posters • automata • victorian books • magic sets
niture • wedgwood pottery • barbecue trays • mexican kitsch • red-clay dinnerware • monterey furnishings
wood carvings • stone carvings • painted walking sticks • beaded suits • redware pottery • wooden signs
e • face jugs • shoshona stonework • painted sticks • easter baskets • depression glass • tarnished silver
rnival chalkware • royal copley pottery • tole trays • staffordshire pottery • majolica • english transferware
s • nutcrackers • mccoy pottery • maple syrup cans • oil paintings • vintage textiles • antique cupboards
ctorian carpet balls • mocha ware • treenware • bandboxes • folk art frames • cocktail shakers • cobalt glass
t chairs • 1940s vases • doll beds • vintage trunks • old postcards • carved hands • toy robots • missouri pine
globes • roseville pottery • red wing pottery • bluebonnet pottery • landscape paintings • texas biedermeier
ooks • state plates • swizzle sticks • japanese ikebana baskets • architectural fragments • looking glasses
sculptures • japanese antiques • italian seating • theatrical posters • automata • victorian books • magic sets
niture • wedgwood pottery • barbecue trays • mexican kitsch • red-clay dinnerware • monterey furnishings
wood carvings • stone carvings • painted walking sticks • beaded suits • redware pottery • wooden signs
e • face jugs • shoshona stonework • painted sticks • easter baskets • depression glass • tarnished silver
rnival chalkware • royal copley pottery • tole trays • staffordshire pottery • majolica • english transferware
s • nutcrackers • mccoy pottery • maple syrup cans • oil paintings • vintage textiles • antique cupboards
ctorian carpet balls • mocha ware • treenware • bandboxes • folk art frames • cocktail shakers • cobalt glass
t chairs • 1940s vases • doll beds • vintage trunks • old postcards • carved hands • toy robots • missouri pine
globes • roseville pottery • red wing pottery • bluebonnet pottery • landscape paintings • texas biedermeier
ooks • state plates • swizzle sticks • japanese ikebana baskets • architectural fragments • looking glasses
sculptures • japanese antiques • italian seating • theatrical posters • automata • victorian books • magic sets
niture • wedgwood pottery • barbecue trays • mexican kitsch • red-clay dinnerware • monterey furnishings
wood carvings • stone carvings • painted walking sticks • beaded suits • redware pottery • wooden signs

1939 world's fair memorabilia • bakelite jewelry • mies van der rohe furniture • lucite handbags • seashells
northwest indian carvings • santos • dog memorabilia • bauer pottery • french dinnerware • haeger potter
horn furniture • native american weaving • rosemaled bowls • metal banks • vintage glass • action figur
southern antiques • architectural drawings • windsor chairs • totem poles • primitive masks • ceremonial bo
photographs • mission furniture • heywood-wakefield furniture • glass paperweights • 1950s italian glas
geometric rugs • western oil paintings • wagon wheels • bottle cap sculpture • psychiatric-patient paintin
cigar-store indians • weather vanes • commercial tins • game boards • beadwork • ceremonial masks • carv
sheet music • red transferware • white dinnerware • figurine pairs • heywood-wakefield furniture • rumrill
bamboo furniture • victorian shell art • cookie jars • orange glass • cigarette boxes • silhouettes • animal
mercury glass • roadside pottery • majolica • french transferware • looking glass • 1930s white pottery • ch
1939 world's fair memorabilia • bakelite jewelry • mies van der rohe furniture • lucite handbags • seashells •
northwest indian carvings • santos • dog memorabilia • bauer pottery • french dinnerware • haeger potter
horn furniture • native american weaving • rosemaled bowls • metal banks • vintage glass • action figur
southern antiques • architectural drawings • windsor chairs • totem poles • primitive masks • ceremonial bo
photographs • mission furniture • heywood-wakefield furniture • glass paperweights • 1950s italian glass
geometric rugs • western oil paintings • wagon wheels • bottle cap sculpture • psychiatric-patient paintin
cigar-store indians • weather vanes • commercial tins • game boards • beadwork • ceremonial masks • carv
sheet music • red transferware • white dinnerware • figurine pairs • heywood-wakefield furniture • rumrill
bamboo furniture • victorian shell art • cookie jars • orange glass • cigarette boxes • silhouettes • animal
mercury glass • roadside pottery • majolica • french transferware • looking glass • 1930s white pottery • ch
1939 world's fair memorabilia • bakelite jewelry • mies van der rohe furniture • lucite handbags • seashells •
northwest indian carvings • santos • dog memorabilia • bauer pottery • french dinnerware • haeger potter
horn furniture • native american weaving • rosemaled bowls • metal banks • vintage glass • action figur
southern antiques • architectural drawings • windsor chairs • totem poles • primitive masks • ceremonial bo
photographs • mission furniture • heywood-wakefield furniture • glass paperweights • 1950s italian glass
geometric rugs • western oil paintings • wagon wheels • bottle cap sculpture • psychiatric-patient paintin
cigar-store indians • weather vanes • commercial tins • game boards • beadwork • ceremonial masks • carv
sheet music • red transferware • white dinnerware • figurine pairs • heywood-wakefield furniture • rumrill
bamboo furniture • victorian shell art • cookie jars • orange glass • cigarette boxes • silhouettes • animal
mercury glass • roadside pottery • majolica • french transferware • looking glass • 1930s white pottery • ch
1939 world's fair memorabilia • bakelite jewelry • mies van der rohe furniture • lucite handbags • seashells •
northwest indian carvings • santos • dog memorabilia • bauer pottery • french dinnerware • haeger potter
horn furniture • native american weaving • rosemaled bowls • metal banks • vintage glass • action figur
southern antiques • architectural drawings • windsor chairs • totem poles • primitive masks • ceremonial bo
photographs • mission furniture • heywood-wakefield furniture • glass paperweights • 1950s italian glass
geometric rugs • western oil paintings • wagon wheels • bottle cap sculpture • psychiatric-patient paintin
cigar-store indians • weather vanes • commercial tins • game boards • beadwork • ceremonial masks • carv